Miracle Moments

Helping the Rescued Become
the Rescuers

by Shawn Abell
and Renée Vajko Srch

Published by Pen It! Publications, LLC in the U.S.A.
812-371-4128   www.penitpublications.com

ISBN: 978-1-952894-92-3
Edited by Wanda Williams
Illustrations by Faythe Payol

Dedication

To all the men and women who have and
continue to serve our country.

Contents

It's not how they were raised,
it's how they survived.

– Shawn Abell –

PROLOGUE

"All you need is love.
Love is all you need."
The Beatles

This book is a collection of stories about a handful of animals among hundreds Shawn Abell has rescued from brutal conditions and certain death. While the content is factual, names – other than the principal subjects – have been changed for privacy purposes. *Dog's Nation* prides itself in maintaining client confidentiality and the stories contained in this book have been written after express permission from those individuals concerned therein.

Dog's Nation also prides itself in matching each individual with the right four-legged companion suited to their needs. Shawn not only trains the dogs but requires each potential handler to participate in the training process in order to learn the behaviors, commands, and tasks their service dog has mastered. Not every dog is fit to be a service dog. Those with health concerns are given alternative roles in supporting communities with needs such as tracking, water safety, 4H programs, as well as serving as ambassadors for *Dog's Nation*.

Owning a service dog does require a diagnosis of autism, PTSD, or other disability, along with a doctor's note confirming the handler's need for assistive medical equipment. Anyone considering a service dog for themselves or for their child should consider the costs involved with owning an animal such as feeding, grooming, and veterinary care. They must accept responsibility for walking, exercising, and feeding their dog as well as assume leadership in order to maintain control of their service dog, thus enabling it to assist through skills taught during training.

For Shawn, it's all about love. Love for dogs and love for those who need a helping hand. That's what *Dog's Nation* is all about.

Chapter One
Miracle

"Where there is great love, there are always miracles."
Willa Cather

The brown terrier was determined to thwart all my efforts at clipping his nails.

"It's okay, Rusty," I said, stroking his paw. "I know you don't like me messing with your nails but we're almost done."

I paused as the shrill ring of the phone broke my concentration, waiting for my receptionist to answer. After the third ring, I let out a groan of frustration.

"Melissa! Can you answer that?" I called out, hoping she was within earshot.

"Got it," my teenage helper grumbled, sauntering past. Stuffing a wad of gum inside her left cheek, Melissa snatched up the receiver. "Hello?"

I shook my head, exasperated. Would that girl ever learn to answer the phone correctly?

"Yes, this is *The Dog's Tale*", Melissa mumbled.

Shifting positions, I stroked Rusty's paw then quickly made a small angled cut. "Good boy, Rusty!" My praise spurred a halfhearted wag of his short, wiry tail. Some dogs enjoy being groomed. Rusty definitely wasn't one of them.

"When?" Melissa said into the phone as she jotted something on a pad of sticky notes. Although I'd downloaded a fairly simple appointment book on my computer, Melissa couldn't seem to get the hang of it.

"Yeah. Okay. Got it. Right. Yep." I'd yet to hear her utter a full sentence.

"Who was that?" I asked when she hung up.

"Some dude. He needs several dogs groomed by Saturday." A small, pink bubble slowly emerged from between her puckered lips, stretching and growing until it popped, pink gum enfolding her mouth. With a quick swipe of her tongue, she peeled the pink goo off her face and tucked it back into her cheek.

With an audible sigh, I handed her the terrier. "Could you put Rusty back in his carrier, then call Mrs. Moss to pick him up at her earliest convenience?"

"Sure thing, Mrs. A." Tucking Rusty under one arm, she pulled her smart phone out of her back pocket and started texting, her fingers flying across the phone's miniature keyboard. I shook my head, wondering how this teenage girl who couldn't even grasp the basics of greeting and scheduling customers could be so proficient with her smart phone.

Slipping into my office which was nothing more than a converted broom closet, I dropped onto the hard, wooden stool behind my desk. Bills, receipts, and order forms spilled from the inbox. My business was doing well and I enjoyed my job as a dog groomer. Yet for some reason, I felt a strong yearning to do something more meaningful with my life. I longed to wake up each morning, knowing I was making a difference and impacting lives for the better.

Peeling the yellow sticky-note off the computer screen, I struggled to decipher Melissa's cryptic note. The name 'Robert' was scrawled across the top, then 'James' beneath it. Were they two separate individuals or just one, I wondered? A phone number, area code 660, suggested the client was calling from Northwest Missouri. Underneath, she'd written 'five-hundred' followed by a dash and the letters SAT, all in caps which she'd circled several times.

"Melissa?" I called out, wandering back to the kennels. I found my receptionist sitting in the lunchroom, feet propped on a chair.

"No way," she said into her phone. "That's so nasty!"

"Melissa," I said, stepping into her line of vision. "I need you to get off the phone."

Melissa frowned, then dropped her feet to the ground. "Yeah. My boss. Later." She tapped her phone, setting it upside down on the table.

I handed her the sticky note. "Can you please clarify this?"

"Some dude named Robert called. That's his call-back number."

"Is it Robert James, James Robert, or are they two different people?" I really needed to hire a suitable replacement. Maybe tomorrow I'd place an ad in the paper.

"I think it's Robert James," she said. "Then again, maybe it's James Robert. He was talking really fast."

"And the five hundred, dash SAT?"

"Dogs. Five hundred dogs. Needs them groomed by Saturday."

I let out a bark of laughter. "Five hundred? You mean five, right?"

"Nope. Five hundred. That's what he said."

"Right," I said, running a hand through my hair. Turning away in frustration, I wandered back to my office and picked up the phone to call James Robert or Robert James, or whoever he was. In the back of my mind, I couldn't help but wonder if this was some teenager's idea of a practical joke. If so, I wasn't amused.

"James and Harris Auction House," a deep voice answered.

"Hello. May I please speak with Robert James?"

"Speaking."

"Hello. This is Shawn Abell, owner of *The Dog's Tale*. My assistant informed me you called." I cleared my throat. "She said you need several dogs groomed by Saturday?"

"Yes, ma'am."

"What breed?"

"'scuse me?"

"What breed are the dogs?"

"Don't rightly know. There's a bit of everything."

"Are most of the dogs long-haired or short-haired?"

"I don't think you understand, ma'am. I have five hundred dogs, all different breeds."

"I - I'm sorry," I stuttered. "Did you say five hundred?"

"Yes, ma'am. Actually, that's just an estimate. There's probably more than that."

"And you need them all groomed by this coming Saturday?"

"That's right. My business partner and I are auctioning off a building this Saturday that was previously owned by a dog breeder. She passed away a couple weeks ago so now we've got a whole mess of dogs we'd like to auction off. Need them cleaned up a bit so they'll fetch a good price..."

Words failed me. This had to be a joke.

While he explained what he needed, I opened my phone directory to the yellow pages, then ran my finger through the As. Accountants, acupuncture, advertising, auction houses. Sure enough, James and Harris Auction House was a legitimate business and the number I'd called matched the one in the directory.

I blew out a lungful of air like a tire that slowly deflates. Five hundred dogs? There was no way I could groom that many in such a short time – unless.

"I need to make a few calls, see if I can recruit a few helpers. I'll get back to you as soon as I can."

"Can you call me by four o'clock? That'll give me enough wiggle room to make other arrangements if you feel you can't do the job."

I bristled. His remark sounded like a taunt. "I can do the job. I just need a little help."

I spent the next hour asking, begging, and shamelessly calling in favors from friends and family.

Finally, I had enlisted enough helpers to get the job done in time.

I called Robert back. "Give me the address and I'll be there bright and early tomorrow morning to provide you with an estimate and hopefully get started with the grooming."

"An estimate?"

"I need to check out the dogs to determine how much time it will take and how much it will cost. Short-haired dogs require a fraction of the time long-haired dogs take. If there are any complications, I …."

"Okay, ma'am. I get the picture." He recited the address, uttered a gruff, "see you tomorrow," then hung up.

For a while, I just sat there, thinking about the daunting task ahead of me. I'd have to reschedule a few clients to the following week but that was a minor detail. The real challenge was in the planning and timely execution of that plan.

Early the next morning, my friend Sarah and I loaded up my Chevy Blazer with shampoos, conditioners, clippers, shears, brushes, dryers, and portable workstation. I hoped to get a jump start by brushing out the long-haired dogs.

The directions Robert had given me led us north, along undulating lanes that rose and dipped through the beautiful Ozarks. Herds of Angus and Charolais dotted the lush green hillocks, contentedly grazing in the warm summer sun. Here and there, combines kicked up a cloud of dust as they cut through fields of sweet, golden corn or sun-ripened soy. I might have enjoyed the drive if I hadn't been so uptight.

"In one hundred feet, turn right onto Woodland Road," my GPS instructed me. I switched on my indicator, then turned right onto a gravel road that meandered past densely wooded acreage. A buzzard, startled by our intrusion, spread its wings, slow and clumsy in its effort to push off the ground and take flight, the remains of some rodent clutched in its strong talons.

"You sure this is right?" my friend Susan asked, checking the address against my GPS.

Squinting against the bright sunlight, I focused on driving. "I sure hope so," I said, skirting another large pothole.

The lane led past a dilapidated barn then humped over a stone bridge spanning a dry creek bed, then curved to the right. A large, metal building suddenly loomed before us, stark and grey against a bright blue sky. The metal roof and walls glimmered under the sun's hot rays. There were no signs or numbers visible on the building.

I frowned, wondering how anyone could house five-hundred dogs inside that one building. "It looks like an airport hangar."

"I would imagine it gets stifling in there during the summer," Sarah said.

I nodded as I stepped out of the car and walked over to the building. I turned the handle, surprised to find the building unlocked. As soon as I pushed the door open, I was hit by sweltering heat and the rank odor of animal waste. I recoiled in horror. Between the smell and the temperature, I was finding it hard to breathe.

"Let's see if they have a back door, we could prop open and get a bit of a breeze blowing through here. If I'd known it was this bad, I could have brought some fans."

Drops of sweat trickled down my back as I walked down the main aisle between the kennels, horrified by the dogs' living conditions. The smaller dogs were confined to cages, so little they could barely turn around or stretch out. Row upon row of those small metal cages lined one side of the building, stacked three high. Along the opposite side of the building, medium to large sized dogs were contained in four-foot chain-link kennels.

It was all too apparent the cages hadn't been cleaned in a while as he stench of urine and feces permeated the building. Some of the dogs showed signs of obvious neglect with open wounds that were bright red and covered in flies. Others lay in their own waste. These dogs would require extensive veterinary care or might even need be put down. This was much more than simple neglect. This was pure evil.

"Let's check the premises, see if they have any warm, running water and fans we can put to good use," I said, tears welling in my eyes.

It was heartbreaking. Some of the younger dogs barked and jumped against the chain link kennels. The older ones just lay there, watching us with doleful eyes as though they'd lost the will to live.

I tried to tell myself these dogs would soon be out of here, hopefully bought by kindhearted individuals who would offer them a good home and a good life. Unfortunately, I knew many of them would simply go to other puppy mills where they would suffer a similar fate.

I was halfway down the aisle when a soft scraping sound caught my attention. Glancing up at one of the cages in the top row, I spotted a young Boston terrier gazing down at me. Black nose pressed against the bars, he pawed at the doors of his prison, begging for attention.

"Hello, little one," I said, as the pup squeezed a foreleg through the bars and pawed the air. A lump rose in my throat. "Yes, I know you want out. Soon, I promise."

Reluctantly, I moved on. So many dogs were sick or covered in feces, it made me want to hurl. Behind me, a choking sound stopped me mid-stride. I turned to look as Sarah's face drained of all color. She was deathly white and swaying as though she were about to keel over. Turning, she rushed out the door, barely dodging the tall, lanky man who was making his way inside, before losing her breakfast in the driveway.

"Miss Abell?" the man said, casting a perplexed glance at Sarah as he stepped through the doorway.

He appeared to be somewhere in his twenties, clean-shaven, and well-dressed. He strode towards me with an air of confidence bordering on cockiness, his cowboy boots thumping loudly on the cement floor.

"That's me," I said, struggling to keep my composure.

"You got an estimate for me?"

"These dogs need to see a vet before I can do anything with them. Some are dying in their own waste. And for Pete's sake, let's get some air going through here. It's way too hot for these poor dogs."

"We got a vet comin'. The ones that are too sick will be put down. Like that one, up there," he said, pointing to the Boston terrier.

"What's wrong with him?" I asked as the pup continued to paw at the bars. I tried not to glance up at him because I couldn't stand to look into those doleful eyes.

"His back legs are pretty messed up. I assume he must have been attacked by some of the other dogs."

Despite myself, my gaze was drawn upward. Gazing into the dog's eyes, I felt a connection with him. He needed me and I needed to help him.

"Can I take him?" I blurted, surprising not only myself but the auctioneer as well.

"Whatcha want him for? He ain't gonna make it, with his legs all tore up."

"It doesn't matter. If I promise to take him to a vet and care for him, will you let me take him? I'll even pay the adoption fee."

He waved away my offer. "You can have 'im, free of charge, if ya want 'im that bad." He frowned. "I gotta git outta here. Stinks somethin' awful."

I had to admit, he did look a little green around the gills.

Immediately, I went in search of a ladder and found one in a back room. Lugging it back to the stack of cages, I set it up, then climbed up so I was level with the little terrier.

"Let's get you out of there," I said, opening the cage. He licked my hand, then started whimpering as I lifted him out. His rear legs hung from scrawny hips, limp and useless, bloody red flesh visible along both thighs.

"What on earth have they done to you?" I whispered, removing my grooming apron.

Gently, I wrapped him in the apron and held him against me. The terrier whimpered softly although I knew he had to be in a considerable amount of pain. Striding out of the building with the dog cradled in my arms, I made my way over to Sarah who was leaning against the car, sipping a can of pop. Although she'd recovered some of her color, she still looked a bit peaked.

"Feel any better?" I asked, laying a hand on her arm.

"A little. The carbonation helped somewhat. But there's no way I'm going back inside that building."

"I won't ask you to. I do, however, think we ought to leave before the vet gets here. He has a gruesome job ahead of him. I'll come back later to do my assessment and estimate."

"What's that?" Sarah asked, pointing to the bundle in my arms.

"A gorgeous Boston terrier I just rescued. They were going to put him down. Robert gave me permission to take him. After all, these dogs are his property now."

Sarah's eyes grew wide. "Let me see him." She tried to pull the apron open but I turned away from her.

"You really don't. His back legs are a mess. Just get in the car and hold him in your lap. Keep him covered, though. I don't want you puking in my car."

Once we got back to El Dorado Springs, I dropped Sarah off at the salon. I could tell from the look on her face that the images from this morning's incident would haunt her for a long time. What we'd witnessed this morning was one of those sights that sticks in your brain for life. From there, I drove straight to the veterinarian's.

He took one look at the terrier and gave it to me straight. "This dog probably won't ever recover from his wounds. There's too much flesh that's exposed and he's in quite a bit of pain. The kindest thing would be to put him to sleep."

"No," I said. "First, I'd like to try a dose of antibiotics, some pain pills, and antibiotic ointment. I'll wash out his wounds every day and keep him away from the other dogs. As long as he's not suffering, I'd like to give him a chance."

The vet didn't seem too keen on the idea but gave in to my wishes. After cleaning the wounds and giving the dog a shot of antibiotics, the vet handed me a vial of pain pills.

"These should help ease the pain. Make sure you wash the wounds every day and keep them clean. Confine him in a separate area, away from your other dogs. I want to see him in two days to evaluate whether or not he's making any progress. Then we'll decide whether to give him that second chance or if we need to put him down."

Back home, I laid the terrier on a little dog bed in the kitchen near the stove. With a child gate to keep the other dogs away, I carefully tended to his wounds using hydro-therapy and antibiotic cream. For the next couple of days, the terrier didn't do much other than eat and sleep. But whenever I came into the kitchen, he'd thump his tail and gaze up at me with eyes that seemed to say, "thank you for saving me."

Two days later, I brought the terrier back to the vet. He was surprised to see how well the wounds were healing.

"You've done a great job with him, Shawn! I'm surprised how healthy the tissue looks."

I was pleased to hear him say that because I'd already grown attached to the little guy. He was sweet-tempered, grateful for every little kindness I showed him, and seemed eager to have another go at life.

Several days later, I came down to breakfast and found the terrier prancing around the kitchen on his front legs, hind legs up in the air. My jaw dropped. "You are just full of surprises, aren't you little guy?"

By now, it seemed likely he would survive his harrowing experience. He was a fighter, a survivor, and every day he showed definite signs of progress. It was time to name him.

"Do you have a particular name in mind?" I asked, squatting down to his level. Tilting his head to one side, the terrier gazed at me as though mulling it over.

"Rex? No, that's too common. You need something special. Angel? No, you really don't look like an angel with your black and white tux. Oh, I don't know. Let me think this through."

As I fixed myself a cup of coffee, I shared my thoughts with my four-legged friend. "You know, it really is a miracle you survived. Even the vet said so."

"Arf!" he barked, his tail whipping back and forth. "Arf!"

Then it hit me. Miracle. That's what he was. A miracle.

"What do you think of the name *Miracle*?"

The little black and white terrier thumped his tail against the tiled floor.

"You like that name?"

His tail thumped harder. "Arf!"

"Then Miracle it is!" I said, laughing.

My little miracle eventually regained full use his back legs, to everyone's astonishment, including the vet's. I taught him to obey simple commands like *sit, stay,* and *lay down. Miracle* was a very intelligent dog, mastering those behaviors so quickly that I continued with his instruction until he was fully trained as a service dog. He graduated with flying colors.

In the process, I discovered how much I enjoyed the time I spent teaching and training the dog. It wasn't just the simple joy that comes from spending quality time with an animal you love. It ran deeper than the pleasure one derives from a hobby. It was a deep happiness and a sense that I was doing something that truly mattered. It was more than a pastime; it was a passion. A passion for saving lives, whether canine or human. Training the dogs I saved to perform specific life-enhancing and life-saving task became my greatest desire.

Miracle was the first of many dogs I rescued from death row. Although I fulfilled my commitment to Mr. James, washing and grooming the dogs whose lives were spared, I decided to sell my business, then founded *Second Chance Barnyard* which eventually became *Dog's Nation*, a non-profit organization that trains and matches service dogs with disabled veterans with physical and/or PTSD as well as individuals diagnosed on the autism spectrum.

Miracles come in various shapes and sizes. Some are blaring and clearly visible, others are small and inconspicuous, but if we look at life with both eyes open, miracles are all around us. Because the gift of life is a miracle in and of itself.

Chapter Two
Jack

"I have found that when you are deeply troubled, there are things you get from the silent devoted companionship of a dog that you can get from no other source."
Doris Day

After rescuing Miracle, I began my life mission of saving and training dogs to become service dogs for disabled individuals in need of physical, mental, and emotional assistance. As shelters, both local and around the country, came to know about *Dog's Nation's*, more and more calls came in asking me to rescue various dogs from brutal conditions or euthanasia. At the same time, my team of volunteers expanded from one to a handful of people who helped clean the kennels, walk, feed, and groom the dogs as well as assist in the training sessions.

Snapshot in hand, I gazed at the young Labrador-mix. He was a beautiful dog, sturdy and well-muscled, with a silky black coat and a wide skull that tapered down to his black nose. When I'd met him at the shelter, he'd struck me as very bright. I'd taken an immediate liking to him and brought him to *Dog's Nation* to train as a service dog.

A loud *bang* off to my right yanked me back to the present. Glancing up from the photo, I noticed a little girl several feet away. She was crying, a limp red balloon dangling from a string clasped tightly in her tiny hand.

Crouching down, her mother wiped away the tears then drew the little girl into a hug. "Oh, honey. I'm so sorry about your balloon. Let's see if we can get you another one, then look for an ice-cream truck? I'm pretty sure I saw one near the merry-go-round."

The little girl sniffled, wiped her nose with the back of her hand, then tottered off, clutching her mother's hand. Smiling, I turned to look at the crowds trickling past the metal barricades near the entrance. Despite the late hour, cars were still pulling into the designated parking area. Music spilled from speakers strung to utility poles, the steady beat of the bass exacerbating the throb in my skull. It didn't help that it was so muggy. My shirt stuck to my back and droplets of sweat trickled down my neck. Last night's rain had brought no relief, only more humidity.

I'd registered for a booth at the El Dorado Springs Annual Picnic to raise awareness about *Dog's Nation*. Many of the dogs we train come from shelters. We make every effort to pair each dog with a new handler, taking into account important criteria such as compatibility, the individual's needs, and the dog's ability to perform required tasks.

My booth was set up near the entrance, away from the heart of the fair where screaming kids, bright lights, and strong odors could send veterans with Post-Traumatic Stress Disorder (PTSD) and individuals on the autism spectrum into a panic attack or a state of high anxiety.

A cluster of boisterous teenagers passed through the barricades, laughing and jostling each other as they headed towards the rides. Behind them, a middle-aged man yanked the bill of his cap lower over his brow. He was dressed in khaki shorts, a black T-shirt, and a cap with *Veteran* stitched on the front. He seemed distraught, his eyes darting left and right as though scanning his surroundings for potential risks. His body was tense, his gait jerky, almost spastic.

Behind him, a slender woman perused the crowd, her gaze coming to rest on the *Dog's Nation* sign propped in front of my booth. "Over here, Joe," she called over her shoulder, making a bee-line towards my table while motioning the man to follow,

I set the Labrador's photo down on the table and offered her a smile. "Hello. May I help you?"

"I hope so," she said. "My brother-in-law told us about *Dog's Nation*. Are you the woman who runs it?"

"Yes, I am," I said, rising to shake the hand she'd extended. "My name is Shawn."

"Kathy. And this is my husband Joe." She turned to address her husband, but he'd covered his ears with his hands. A sheen of sweat spread across his brow, his face creased in pain.

A rush of compassion filled my chest. This man had risked his life for his country, yet that sacrifice came at a great cost as it did for so many of our veterans.

"The noise bothers him quite a bit," Kathy said.

"I understand. It does get pretty loud. Did your husband serve overseas?"

"Yes. He served in Iraq. In the Air Force. Unfortunately, he suffers from PTSD. It has grown progressively worse over the past several months. He's given up sleeping in bed because of night terrors that wake him every hour or so. Instead, he watches TV until he falls asleep on the couch. He won't go out anymore, doesn't eat meals with me and the kids,

34

won't even go to church with us. It was quite the challenge to get him to come with me today."

I glanced over at Joe. His gaze was fixed on the picture of the dog I'd just set down on the table. It rested on top of several other photos of dogs I was currently training.

"Are you needing a service dog?" I asked.

The man nodded. "My wife –."

His words were cut short by a *bang*. Instantly, Joe ducked and covered his head with both arms. He was shaking, his breath raspy and shallow. Loud noises, like the one we'd just heard, often took veterans back to the war zones, their minds reliving the terrors of the constant shooting and bombs exploding.

"It's a balloon," I told the couple, recognizing the sound. "The same thing happened a short while ago and it scared the bejeebers out of me."

Slowly, the man straightened up, his eyes wide with fear. "I... I'm sorry. I thought –."

"Joe desperately needs help," his wife said. I recognized that look of despair I've seen in the eyes of so many veterans and veterans' spouses.

"Is this one available?" Joe asked, pointing to the photo of the black Labrador.

"One of several. This one is a black Lab-mix. Great temperament. Smart."

"We'll take him," Joe blurted.

I was taken aback by his words. He hadn't even asked how old the dog was, how long it would take to train him, or if he would be suited to his needs.

"Are you sure? I have several dogs I'm working with," I said, spreading out the photos on the table.

"I want this one," Joe said. "What's its name?"

"I've just recently adopted him, so I haven't really decided yet. Why don't you come over to *Dog's Nation* so you two can meet and we'll see if you're compatible?"

"Jack. His name is Jack." Apparently, Joe had already made up his mind he wanted this particular dog. Sometimes, it happens that way. There's an instant connection and I always try to honor that.

"Jack was his battle buddy in Iraq," Kathy told me.

"Then Jack it is," I said.

"Is he ready for adoption?" Kathy asked.

"I'll need to do an assessment first, in order to determine Joe's specific needs. I also need a doctor's note stating Joe requires the assistance of a service dog. After that, I can do further training with Jack to be certain he is capable of meeting all of Joe's needs."

"How long will that take?"

"Typically, it takes six to seven months, depending on the dog and the precise tasks he will need to master."

"Six months? But Joe has his heart set on attending a Betty Boop Fly Show."

"When is that?" I asked.

She told me the date.

"I'll do my best to have Jack ready by then, but it really depends on the dog and how quickly it learns what is needed."

After filling out the proper forms, I handed Jack's photo to Joe. I prayed they would be a good match because Joe really seemed to have his heart set on this dog.

Thankfully, Jack was an extremely smart canine. I took him to the community center where I trained him how to go up the stairs, one step ahead of me in order to provide support should Joe lose his balance. I taught him to go down the stairs, one step at a time, on the same step beside me, ready to provide stability should his handler lose his balance. I taught Jack how to brace, in case Joe required support. I trained him how to 'cover' his handler by standing behind Joe, blocking the public from coming up from behind and tapping Joe on the shoulder which could induce a panic attack. Jack learned to perform an 'all clear parameter check" so no one crowded Joe or moved in too close. Jack had to learn to ride the elevator, to focus on his handler and not get distracted by people, odors, or other animals. I exposed Jack to crowds, trained him how to enter and exit church pews, how to walk alongside a shopping cart, how to cope with various floor surfaces, especially the bigger stores where fluorescent lights reflect off the linoleum and sometimes frighten dogs. I taught him many other tasks that are part of the basic training required for service dogs as well as those specific to Joe's physical and mental needs.

Finally, after months of training, Jack graduated and was ready to move to his new home. Because Joe had visited often and worked with Jack, learning the commands and bonding through play, the transition was fairly easy. Jack knew his purpose in life and seemed eager to get started.

Several months later, I received a very special photo; Joe and Kathy had made it to the Betty Boop Fly Show, posing in front of a blue and yellow Cessna, Jack sitting proud and tall beside Joe, sporting his service dog vest. That photo went on my victory wall, a reminder that *Dog's Nation* was changing lives, one dog and one person at a time.

With Jack's help Joe was able, to a certain extent, to reintegrate into society and handle social interactions in a healthier manner. Having a dog to care for meant Joe had to take him out when nature called, needed to walk the dog twice a day, as well as groom and feed him. This new responsibility gradually pulled Joe out of the darkness where he'd been living for so long. His mood also improved as his mind slowly began to heal.

Joe went back to sleeping upstairs with his wife. The night terrors became less frequent and not as severe because of Jack's presence beside him. He rejoined his wife and kids at the kitchen table, enjoying those precious moments he could spend with his family. He regained some of his confidence, taking his kids shopping for new clothes, attending Sunday morning services with his family, and even inviting some of his buddies over for a meal.

When he felt himself slipping back into a dark mood, Joe would take Jack out to the back yard and play catch or tug-of-war with Jack's stuffed toys. And even though Joe still suffered occasional nightmares and anxiety, Jack's presence shortened their duration and intensity. Jack truly was Joe's best friend.

One morning, late the next fall, I received a call from Kathy.

"Shawn, this is Kathy." Her voice cracked; immediately, I sensed something terrible had happened.

"Hi Kathy. Is Jack okay?"

"Jack is fine. He's been such a help to Joe. I…" A sob caught in her throat and my heart plummeted. "I just called to tell you Joe passed away some time during the night. When he didn't come down for breakfast, our daughter went up to check on him. She found her dad lifeless, Jack curled up beside him. Joe must have slipped away peacefully because Jack never made a sound."

"Oh, Kathy. I'm so sorry." My words seemed so shallow. After all, what do you say to those who are left behind, those who are grieving and have lost a huge part of their lives?

"I just wanted to say thank you," Kathy said.

"For what?"

"For Jack. And for giving Joe back to us for a time."

A lump formed in my throat as I fought my own tears.

"Jack is the one you need to thank. He did most of the work."

"If you don't mind, we'd like to keep Jack. He's part of our family now."

"Of course."

"His presence will constantly remind us of the precious time we had with Joe."

Another sob, then a click on the other end of the line. Kathy had hung up. I settled the receiver back in its cradle and swiped at the tears trickling down my cheeks. Yet despite my sadness, a smile played on my lips as I remembered Joe posing in front of that Cessna at the Betty Boop Fly Show and the smile that lit up his face. Jack had provided that devoted companionship and healing Joe had so desperately needed.

Chapter Three
Charm

*"Dogs have a way of finding the people who need them,
and filling an emptiness we didn't ever know we had."*
Thom Jones

Standing at the kitchen window, sipping my first cup of coffee, I watched as a soft tangerine sunrise bled across the eastern sky, promising another beautiful day in the Ozarks. I loved these early morning moments when the world was still waking to warm, golden sunlight and the day held promise and untold possibilities.

A large van turned into my drive, winding its way slowly towards the house. *Must be the Clarks,* I thought, kicking off my slippers and stepping into a pair of rubber boots. Mr. Clark had called me several weeks ago about adopting a service dog for their son, Matthew, a twelve-year old boy with autism spectrum disorder.

"Matthew has no sense of danger," his father told me over the phone. "He'll wander off on his own, oblivious to the world around him. We've installed locks on the doors, but they're useless. He finds other ways to get out and before you know it, some neighbor calls us to let us know they spotted Matthew wandering down the road. My wife and I take turns keeping watch day and night but we're exhausted. We haven't slept properly in years."

After talking at length with the boy's parents, assessing his specific needs, and requesting a note from his doctor certifying Matthew needed a service dog, I selected Charm to be his partner.

I'd adopted Charm, a gorgeous golden retriever, from a nearby shelter. She would be a good fit for this active, high-strung, twelve-year-old boy. Not only was Charm a sweet-natured dog, she was also smart, quick, and energetic. At six months of age, she'd already received her Canine Good Citizenship certification. This is a nationally recognized program that introduces dogs to certain behaviors such as sitting on command, staying put, and responding appropriately to basic commands.

"Hello," the boy's father called out, stepping out of the van. "Miss Abell, I presume?"

"Yes," I said, shaking hands with him. "You must have set out quite early to make it here by sunrise."

"It was a tad early," he chuckled. "But we're all so excited to meet Matthew's new dog, we didn't mind. My name's Bob, by the way, and this is my wife, Priscilla."

A petite woman stepped from the van and nodded in my direction, as though dredging up a smile required too much energy. Her thick, auburn locks were pulled back in a messy knot at the back of her head and heavy bags underlined both eyes.

Behind her, a gaggle of kids poured from the van, ranging from teens to toddlers. They were quiet and well behaved, nodding as each one was introduced. Bringing up the rear was Matthew. Tall for his age and extremely thin, the boy stared at the ground, his hands flapping at his sides as he rocked back and forth.

"Hello, Matthew," I said. "I have a special dog I'd like you to meet. May I bring her out so you can get to know her?"

The boy nodded, our eyes barely connecting before he turned away.

"Okay. Wait here while I go fetch her."

As soon as Charm saw me coming around the corner of the house, she rushed to greet me, pushing her nose through the chain link fence around her kennel. This energetic dog was always ready for an adventure or a romp in the park. She would be perfect for an overactive child.

"You ready to meet your boy?" I asked, opening the gate to her kennel and clipping on her lead.

"Woof," she said, her tail swishing back and forth like a metronome.

Trotting gracefully by my side, Charm rounded the house. But as soon as she spotted the kids, her demeanor changed. Her tail swished faster, her pace picked up, and she let out a deep 'woof.' Charm loved kids.

"Matthew, I'd like you to meet Charm. She wants to be your friend."

I was anxious to assess the connection between the two. Would Matthew respond to the dog or ignore her? Would Charm bond with her new handler? Any concerns I might have entertained vanished when Matthew saw Charm. Instantly, he stopped stimming and his face broke into a big smile. Kneeling beside the golden retriever, the boy wrapped his arms gently around her broad neck and shoulders. Undaunted by this sudden show of affection, Charm leaned into the boy, then licked his face.

"I think it's a match," I said, smiling. "Would you like to hold her leash and walk her around the yard a bit?"

Matthew cast a glance my way, then nodded. I handed Matthew the leash, instructing him how to walk his dog and what to say if he wanted her to stop, sit, or lay down.

"One of things you mentioned is that you have quite a bit of livestock," I said to his parents as we stood together, watching Matthew and Charm bond.

"That's right. We have cattle, chickens, pigs, and ducks."

"That is something I will definitely have to work on. Charm requires a bit more training, and I am also teaching her a behavior called 'anchoring' which will prevent Matthew from running off or dashing into traffic. All this will take a few weeks."

"So, we can't take the dog today?" his mother asked. She looked so disappointed.

"Not right away, no. Today we will simply assess how well Matthew and Charm bond and whether Matthew can master the commands I've taught Charm. I also want to evaluate Matthew's needs so I can train Charm to meet those specific requirements. Let's go into town where we can see how the two of them do in a public setting. If you'll follow me, the park is just a few miles away."

The father nodded. "Certainly. Come on kids, back into the van."

Matthew let out a wail of protest as I took Charm's lead and walked her to my car.

"It's okay, Matthew, it's okay," his mother said. "We're going to the park where you can walk Charm and play with her. For now, she's riding in Miss Shawn's car but you'll see her again in a few minutes."

Reluctantly, he climbed back into the van. I could see him sitting way in the last seat, his fingers entwined in his hair, yanking on it. I'd have to train Charm how to interrupt those self-harming behaviors.

Once downtown, I handed Matthew the leash, watching as he and the dog strolled around the park together, Matthew's tip-toed gait so typical of autism.

"Matthew looks so pleased," his mother said, softly. "I can't remember the last time I've seen him smile."

I nodded. "Moments such as these are what make all the long hours of training so worthwhile."

I spent the rest of the day working with Matthew and Charm. The boy was quick to learn the commands I'd taught Charm who, in turn, responded well to Matthew's instructions. Team Charm was a go.

The weeks following Matthew's visit were busy. I exposed the dog extensively to an array of farm animals, training her not only to leave them be but also to ignore them when she was in her harness. Charm had to stay focused on her job and couldn't be distracted by a lamb bleating or a chicken running wild. Any prey-drive she might have harbored as a young dog was overpowered by her desire to obey and please which is exactly what I'd aimed for.

I took her to church and taught her how to navigate pews and lay silently by my feet during the service. I trained her on de-escalating techniques should Matthew have a meltdown and taught her how to interrupt self-harming behaviors such as hair-pulling.

But the biggest part of our training time was spent teaching her to 'anchor.' Anchoring is a technique where the child is tethered to his service dog with a special harness. If the child starts to run, the dog sits down and braces herself, preventing the child from wandering any further than the length of the tether, thus 'anchoring' the child until his parents can take over. Anchoring ensures the child's safety by preventing him from running into traffic or taking off in a crowd.

The day Matthew came to fetch Charm was cold and dreary. This time, only his mother and baby brother accompanied him. I had hoped for some sun to brighten my mood but it turned out, I didn't require the sun's help. All I needed was to see

Matthew jump out of the van as soon as it pulled to a stop in front of my house, yelling "Charm! Charm!" to boost my spirits and warm my heart. Charm would be going to a good home, one where she would be loved and cherished. In gifting this dog to Matthew, I would be saving two lives instead of just one.

"Yes, Charm is ready for you to take home," I said, smiling at Matthew. "Wait here while I fetch her."

It was all the boy could do to contain himself. Bouncing up and down, he let out a squeal of excitement. As I rounded the house and headed to the kennels out back, I could hear him chanting, "Charm" over and over.

Charm was more than ready to go home with her boy. This was her big day. She knew her mission in life was to care for and protect this young boy and she was eager to get started. As soon as I returned with the dog, Matthew cried out, "Charm!" and ran to her, dropping to his knees so he could wrap his arms around her. Charm licked his ear, generating a burst of laughter from her boy. This was a good day, indeed.

"Charm. Charm. Charm," Matthew repeated, over and over, enamored of this dog who had stolen his heart.

His mom and I alternately laughed and cried as we witnessed something very special happening between this boy and his dog. Sometimes, the best remedy for whatever ails you walks on four paws. I know because I've seen it time and again. I wished them well, gave Charm a kiss good-bye, then waved them off. Matthew was sitting in the very last seat in the back, Charm right beside him, a big smile on the boy's face. If I cried, they were tears of happiness.

Several days later, Matthew's mom called to give me an update.

"You won't believe what happened," she said. Her voice was bright and bubbly, so different from the woman I'd met weeks ago. "Charm has worked miracles. During the trip back to Arkansas we stopped at a fast-food restaurant to grab a bite to eat. For the first time, I was able to take the baby into the restroom to change his diaper without having to take Matthew in with me. You have no idea how embarrassing it is to drag a twelve-year-old boy into the women's restroom. This time, I sat Matthew down at a table with Charm on her lead. When I came out, Matthew was right where I'd left him."

"That's wonderful," I was thrilled. Charm was doing precisely what she was trained to do.

"Wait! It gets even better," his mom went on. "We stopped at a store to grab a few groceries before heading home. Instead of lagging like he usually does, Matthew walked ahead of me and the baby, head held high, Charm padding along beside him. No stimming, no staring at the ground. It's as if he's gained a new sense of confidence."

"I'm so happy for him. And for you. Sounds like Charm has made quite the difference."

"Shawn, we can never thank you enough for the wonderful gift you gave us. Now that Charm is here to keep an eye on our son, my husband and I will be able to breathe a lot easier."

"And sleep with both eyes shut," I added, laughing.

Chapter Four
Hidden Angel

"Some angels have four legs and fur."
Author Unknown

"Hello?" The voice on the other end of the line was terse. "Is this Shawn?"

"Ye-e-e-e-s," I replied warily as I struggled to clear the cobwebs of slumber from my mind. Glancing at the bright red numbers on my alarm clock, I noticed it was barely six a.m.

"This is Sue."

My mind strived to match a face with the name but came up empty. One of my friends was named Susan, but this woman's voice sounded nothing like hers.

"I'm one of the first responder for St. Clair county," she said.

Finally, the penny dropped. I sat up and rubbed the sleep from my eyes.

"I'm about to head over to a property just off Highway 54," she continued. "A concerned citizen called last night to report a case of animal neglect. Apparently, her neighbor bought a mare at an auction, but he hasn't been 'round in a long time to check on her."

A mixture of anger and pity welled up within me. Anger at the owner, pity for the poor mare. I fail to understand why people take in animals, only to neglect them. This irresponsible attitude towards pets has become an epidemic in Missouri, one which needs to be addressed without delay.

"Give me the address and I'll go take a look," I said, grabbing the pen and notepad I kept beside my bed. Considering I'm on call twenty-four/seven, receiving a phone call at all hours of the night is not uncommon.

After jotting down directions, I agreed to meet her there in an hour. Running a hand through my hair, I fought the urge to scream. A starving horse was not on the day's agenda. Then again, most of the animals I take in are last-minute surprises.

Shuffling to the kitchen, I poured water into the coffee maker, then scooped enough grounds for two cups. There wouldn't be any more sleep for me today. The hot coffee helped clear my head. I wasn't too sure what I would be up against today and needed to be alert and quick on my feet. A frightened horse could potentially be dangerous.

After a quick shower and a call to a friend who owns a truck and cattle trailer, I headed out. Darkness had yielded to a glorious sunrise, hues of salmon, rose, and lavender stretching across the early morning sky. I paused for a moment, soaking in the stunning sight, strains of Louis Armstrong's song, "What a Wonderful World" playing through my mind. I needed to permeate my mind and my soul with this image in order to tackle the disturbing prospect which lay ahead.

A nippy autumn breeze snuck through the thin fibers of my sweater as I trudged towards my car, hands wrapped around a travel mug filled with coffee. Russet-colored leaves crackled under my boots. Soon the autumn rains would arrive, washing away the beautiful sun-kissed colors of fall, leaving bare trees and soggy leaves in its wake.

Despite the fact that I was driving into the sun, I was able to find the place fairly easily. A rusty barb wire fence encircled the small property. Several trees had been stripped of their bark, leading me to think the mare had been scouring for food for quite some time. I could only hope the tree bark hadn't torn up her digestive track.

Slipping quietly from my vehicle, I craned my neck for a glimpse of the horse. All I could see was mud, dried leaves, and overgrown weeds. The sharp, shrill screech of a hawk soaring overhead pierced the morning silence, its broad, rust-colored chest evident in the bright morning sunlight.

The crunch of tires on gravel startled me. I spun around to see my friend John pulling up with his truck and trailer. Behind him came a grey pickup.

"Are you Shawn?" the driver said, stepping from her truck. She was average height, with long, truffle-brown hair tied in a loose ponytail, and a deep, gravelly voice. Her slender face stood out in stark contrast to her wide shoulders and sturdy build.

I nodded. "Yes, I'm Shawn."

Sue offered her hand in greeting. "Thanks for coming on such short notice."

"Of course. I've been trying to spot the mare you called about but haven't seen any movement. You sure she's still in there?"

"Gotta be. Neighbor said she had to untangle the poor creature from the barb wire last night. Cut the mare up pretty good, apparently. She might be hiding among the tall weeds at the back of the property. Let's go in."

Saving animals is not for the faint of heart. This certainly proved true in this case. My hands clenched into fists as we came upon the mare, concealed behind a mess of tall weeds. The poor girl had angry, red sores across her back and both flanks. Despite the flies swarming around her, the mare made no move to swish them away with her tail. She looked like a skeleton draped in a thin brown sheet. Beside her, lay a dead foal.

I was speechless, shocked by the owner's cruelty. How could any human being leave a mare and her foal to starve to death? A lump formed in my throat and I suddenly found it hard to swallow. I wanted to punch a wall, to release my pent-up fury. Instead, I sucked in a deep, calming breath, then slowly approached the mare, trying to lock eyes with her so she could see I meant her no harm.

I gasped when her head swiveled in my direction; only the whites of her eyes showed, veiled by a thick, greyish film. The poor mare was blind.

"Hey, there, sweetie," I cooed, trying to infuse some reassurance into my voice. For all I knew, she might be terrified of strangers, especially ones she couldn't see.

Steeling myself for the worst, I took another step. The mare didn't shy away or rear up. Instead, she offered a faint whicker. Reaching up, I gently stroked her long, white mane. It was a tangled mess, caked with dirt and bits of dried leaves.

"I'm here to help you, sweetheart," I said, in a soothing voice. "I'm here to take you to your new home."

Sue had pulled out her phone and was talking to someone about fetching the dead foal. I was glad to be spared that gruesome task.

"Come on, girl," I said, coaxing the mare to trust me.

She obviously sensed my good intentions, for she allowed me to slip a halter over her head and lead her through the cloying mud and out onto the gravel road. Together, Sue and I managed to get her up the ramp and into the trailer, fastening her lead to a ring inside to steady her for the ride.

"Thank you, Sue," I said. "I'm glad you called me."

"I'm just relieved you came out right away," she said, shaking her head. "I'm not sure she would have lasted much longer."

Back at the farm, Joe and I offloaded the mare. "Welcome home, sweet girl," I said, guiding her to the pasture she would call home from now on.

After I'd removed the halter, the mare began walking in circles. I cast a worried look at John.

"I think she's trying to get her bearings," he said.

"I guess."

John shrugged. "She'll figure it out. Guess I'll be gettin' on home if you don't mind."

"Thanks for your help, John. I really appreciate it."

It didn't take long for Hidden Angel — that's what I began to call her and the name stuck — to settle in to her new home. After a visit from the vet and several sponge baths with medicated water, her sores began to heal. As she grew stronger and more secure in her new setting, she slowly revealed her sweet, if sometimes cheeky, nature.

One morning, about two weeks after I'd brought her home, I stood gazing out the kitchen window. My gorgeous tobiano fox trotter was running circles, as was her habit, whinnying with joy. She'd put on a bit of weight and her sores were no longer as noticeable. Her beautiful mane, once so dirty and grey, was now pure white and flowed gracefully between her broad shoulders.

"Beautiful angel," I whispered, a smile tugging at my lips.

Stepping over to the coffee maker I flipped it on, then returned to the window to watch the mare while it brewed. Hidden Angel had come to a halt, her face turned towards the house. She'd heard me turn on the coffee pot! Trotting towards her food dish, she nudged it until it rattled.

I burst into laughter, then cranked open the kitchen window. "I know, I know. You want your breakfast."

She whinnied loudly and rattled her dish again. Hidden Angel was on the mend, both inside and out. She was spirited and feisty and, though she still bore the scars of neglect and abuse, she would pull through just fine.

Hidden Angel has brought so much joy into my life. She is gentle, friendly, loving, and loyal. My heart wells with gratitude that Sue called me in time. So often, saving animals is a grueling and thankless task. But loving them and knowing they love me in return is reward enough.

Chapter Five
Roxy

*"Accept the challenges so that you can
feel the exhilaration of victory."*
George S. Patton

"She's paralyzed," my friend Susan told me over the phone.

"Paralyzed?" I wasn't quite sure how to respond as I tried to wrap my mind around the word. After all, what do you say when someone calls and asks if you'll take a Dachshund who can't walk?

"She has a wheel-chair and a drag bag," Susan added, as though that might influence my decision.

A dog wheelchair is an apparatus with a pair of wheels that line up with the dog's back legs. The wheelchair offers support while the dog's front legs provide the mobility. A drag bag is a wearable nylon sack which allows the dog to pull itself around the house when it's not strapped in the wheel-chair.

"What happened to her?"

"She's pedigreed, so her owners decided to breed her," Susan said. "She had one litter, but she had a difficult labor which proved too much for her and ended up with partial paralysis. Her owners took her to a veterinary surgeon but the operation wasn't successful. Both owners work all day, which means the dog is home alone most of the time. That's hard on any dog, let alone one that's paralyzed. They asked if I knew someone who might be able to offer her a better life than what they can offer her. I immediately thought of you."

I admit, I was a bit hesitant. My mind was running through all the ramifications. I had all I could handle at the present time and wouldn't have much time to work with her. But my heart won out. I knew I had to take her. I couldn't turn away a dog simply because the timing wasn't convenient.

"Okay. Where is this dog?" I grabbed pen and paper to jot down directions.

"She lives in California. But the owners' son is flying into Kansas City to visit a friend, so he offered to drop her off."

It came as a relief to hear the dog was coming to me instead of the other way around. I often find myself trying to decipher my scribbles and abbreviations as I drive along dark country roads that don't show up on any GPS.

"He's flying in tomorrow, which means he'd arrive at your house around 7 p.m."

"O-kay," I said, dragging out the syllables as my mind tried to adjust to this bit of news. "You told them I'd take the dog before checking with me, didn't you?"

Susan was silent, confirming my suspicions. Once again, she'd counted her chicks before they'd hatched.

"It's okay, Susan. What's the dog's name?"

"Roxy. Her owners told me she's quite the little gal. Loving, adventurous, and full of life, despite her handicap."

Deep down, Susan and I knew this was where Roxy belonged. After all, *Dog's Nation* is all about helping those with impairments.

"Can't wait to meet her," I said. "Thanks for thinking of me."

"You're quite welcome, Shawn." I could hear the amusement in Susan's voice. "After all, isn't that what friends are for?"

The next evening Roxy arrived, cradled in the arms of a tired-looking young man. "Hi, I'm Steve," he said, setting the dog's carrier along with a bag by the front door. "And this is Roxy. Her wheels and drag cloth are in the bag, along with her toys, her bed, and her favorite blanket."

Steve looked away as he gently stroked the dog's soft ears. "Mom and Dad were in tears when they saw us off, but we all know this is for the best." I could hear raw emotion in his voice. This was just as difficult on him as it was on his parents.

"Hello, Roxy," I said, stroking her smooth, black coat. She was a gorgeous Brindle Dachshund, with tan points along her nose and paws.

"Ark! Ark! Ark!" she replied, setting off a chorus of barks in the bedroom. I'd temporarily banished my four-legged entourage to my room so Roxy wouldn't feel so overwhelmed.

Steven pulled her drag cloth from the bag, slipped it on, then set her on the floor. Immediately, she dragged herself across the living-room, sniffing the rug and furniture like a good hunting dog.

"Well, I guess I'd better get going. Still have a long drive ahead of me," Steven said, swiping at his eyes. "Thanks again for taking her in."

"My pleasure," I said, walking him to the door. "I promise to take good care of her. Safe travels."

From the front porch, I watched him drive away, then hurried back into the house. My foursome was raising a ruckus in the bedroom, barking and baying like hounds on a hunt. Roxy had dragged herself all the way to the bedroom and was snuffling the narrow gap under the door.

"Roxy, are you causing trouble already?" I said, chuckling as I scooped up the little dog and settled her in the crook of my arm. "Let's get you some water and a bite to eat, shall we?"

Thankfully, the other dogs readily accepted her into their midst. Despite her unusual needs, Roxy settled in quite nicely. The day after her arrival, I took her to meet Hidden Angel. She started yapping as soon as she saw the horse, catching Hidden Angel's attention. The mare followed the sound of my voice and Roxy's yapping until she and the dog were touching noses over the fence. The two immediately struck up an uncanny friendship. It was as though they shared a special bond; a blind horse and a paralyzed dog who'd both been blessed with a second chance at life.

Roxy wasn't a quiet, lazy sort of dog. On the contrary, she faced life head-on, seemingly unperturbed by her limited mobility. She would tear around the property, visiting with Hidden Angel or chasing after the cats. If her wheels got stuck in the mud or in brambles, she'd howl for help then take off again as soon as I extricated her. She rapidly claimed her own spot on my bed, next to my pillow, unfazed by the close proximity of my other dogs, most of whom were three to four times her own size and weight. What she lacked in size and ability, she made up in courage, determination, and pure stubbornness. No one, and I mean no one, was going to stop her from doing whatever she'd set her mind to.

She could also be quite demanding. When she finished eating, she would cry out in a yodel-like warble, her signal for me to come fetch her, as though I didn't have anything to do other than fetch and carry all day long. She seemed to view me as her personal butler. If I didn't respond quickly enough, she'd grow bored and get into mischief.

I started taking her with me when I went out, just to keep her out of trouble. One of her favorite outings was when she and I visited with the boys and girls from the local school's special education class. Roxy and I would meet them at the park on Fridays where they went for their weekly class outing. To say the kids loved her would be an understatement. She was their friend as well as their inadvertent mentor. She inspired them to tackle their own impediments, to persevere no matter the obstacles, and enjoy life to the fullest.

The first few months, our outings were contained to controlled environments. But as Roxy thrived, I began to include her in our excursions to festivals and fairs. When she was two years old, I signed her up to be a part of our town's 4th of July parade. Her participation, along with the other dogs

I'd registered for the event, was intended to help raise awareness about *Dog's Nation* and service dogs in general. But the day of the parade, Roxy seemed skittish and uncooperative. At first, I thought she wasn't feeling well or was afraid of the crowd. She resisted my efforts to strap her into her wheelchair and once I finally succeeded, she reacted by flipping her wheels and refusing to walk. I finally picked her up and carried her, disappointed by her non-compliance. I had really been hoping she would inspire many people with her bold defiance in the face of adversity. Little did I know that would be the last time she used her wheelchair.

Home once more, I set her down on ground.

"What was that about?" I said, offering her a bowl of cold water. "It's not the first time you've been in a parade, so what gives?"

I was about to turn away and go back inside when I suddenly noticed her tail twitching.

"Look!" I gasped, grabbing James' arm. He's one of the volunteers who works at *Dog's Nation*. "She's moving her tail!"

James and I squealed in delight and danced a little jig on my patio. As we danced, red, white, and blue fireworks lit up the sky.

"Look, Roxy!" I said, laughing. "They're celebrating you!"

It was a small victory, but a victory, nonetheless.

The following day, a news crew came to film a report about the work we were doing at *Dog's Nation*. I was in the middle of explaining our mission statement, when James exclaimed, "Shawn!"

We all turned to look at him, then glanced where he was pointing. Roxy was walking! This dachshund, who'd been paralyzed for two years, was taking small, hesitant steps. Tears trickled down my cheeks as I witnessed this unexpected miracle.

"She's been paralyzed for two years but now she's walking," I told the reporter as I watched in amazement."

"Did you catch that?" the reporter asked the camera man who wasn't sure whether he should focus on the dog or my tear-stained face.

The next day, I took Roxy to an acupuncturist. She was shocked. "I have no idea how she's able to walk. All her muscles in the rear have wasted away. There's no scientific explanation. I can only say, it's a miracle."

Word quickly spread about Roxy's unexplainable recovery. Of course, everyone who knew her was delighted, especially the children in the special-education class.

"How come she can walk now, Miss Shawn?" a little boy named Colton asked, pulling on my pant leg.

"Did God make her all better?" ten-year old Jennifer asked, shyly.

I didn't have the answers, only proof that miracles happen even when we least expect them.

Now that she could get around on her own, Roxy was even more adventurous and daring, exploring ditches she couldn't reach in her wheelchair, sniffing out rabbits and chasing them across the fields. She scented out a family of raccoons that had taken up residence at the far end of the property and chased them off the premises. Roxy was unstoppable.

Eventually, it was her heart that put a stop to Roxy's escapades. She'd had heart issues for a while so I assumed she'd died of heart failure when I woke up one morning to find her motionless little body snuggled up against my pillow. She'd passed peacefully in her sleep, aged fifteen. We buried her under her favorite dogwood tree where she loved to sleep in its shade and planted an American flag to mark her grave. Her death left a big void in our lives. Even Hidden Angel seemed affected by her absence. But even though Roxy was no longer with us, she still had one final gift to offer.

A couple of months after her passing, my pastor friend called, asking if I knew where to get a wheelchair for his dachshund who'd started experiencing weakness in his back legs.

"Absolutely! Stop by whenever you get the chance. I have Roxy's wheelchair just waiting for the right candidate."

My pastor friend had known Roxy, had even held her and made a fuss of her every time I'd visited his church.

"How fitting," he said. "Even after her death, Roxy is still influencing lives for the better."

Chapter Six
Maverick

*"Maverick is a word which appeals to me more than misfit.
Maverick is active, misfit is passive."*
Alan Rickman

Maverick wasn't the type to be limited by a handicap. To him, challenges were nothing more than hurdles that had to be cleared. If he couldn't jump over those obstacles, he'd find a way to crawl under them or scamper around them. It was all the same to him. It was that independent spirit and live-life-to-the-fullest attitude that served him in good stead when his back leg had to be amputated. Despite, maybe even because of, his limitations, Maverick has been one of my best representatives for disabilities. Let me share his story with you.

I'd been looking at options, trying to find ways to recruit more volunteers to help at *Dog's Nation*. What I needed the most were individuals who could walk the dogs and hold them on a lead while I worked individually with each dog, training them in public settings. One of those venues was a safe house near the center of town, that welcomed women and children who were trying to get back on their feet after leaving abusive home situations. Walking the dogs was beneficial to the children, especially, as it offered them an opportunity to get outside, get some exercise, and interact with animals which is therapeutic in and of itself.

One day, I received a call from a local veterinarian about a fawn-colored pit bull who'd broken out of a fenced-in yard. He'd been hit by a car while running across a busy highway. One of his back legs had multiple broken bones that required extensive surgery. Sadly, his owner couldn't afford the surgical fees. The vet wanted to know whether or not I would take him and pay for the surgery or if he should put the dog down.

"He's fairly young and quite healthy other than the broken leg," the veterinarian informed me over the phone. "He's very friendly and outgoing. Sharp mind too. Seems a shame to put him down."

After talking at length with the vet, I agreed to pay for the surgery as long as I could officially adopt the dog. Once everything was set, Maverick went to surgery. Although the operation itself went well, Maverick didn't like his cast or being confined in order to rest his leg. He wanted to be up and about, taking walks with the other dogs, and chasing balls.

After the cast was removed, Maverick continued to have troubles. He had an obvious limp and seemed to favor his hind leg. I followed up with the veterinarian, then took him to get acupuncture treatments and physical therapy, but the boisterous, fun-loving dog gradually lost all ability to bear weight on that leg. About a year after his surgery, a bone infection set in. There were no options left other than to amputate the leg.

But having only three legs instead of four didn't seem to faze Maverick. He still ran with the other dogs, played fetch, and kept up with the pack.

By this time, I had befriended a young woman and her three children who were staying in the shelter for abused woman. When their mother was eventually arrested and incarcerated, C.J. and his sisters came to stay with me until she was released. Maverick absolutely loved to play with the kids and kept a close eye on them whether indoors or outdoors. The kids were delighted to be able to spend as much time as they wanted with the dogs, instead of just the few hours they usually spent with them on Wednesday afternoons; especially Maverick.

In many ways, Maverick reminded me of a doting, yet playful parent. Sometimes I would find one of the kids sitting on the sofa, Maverick sitting with his head cocked to the side as they poured out their heartache to him. He would lay in the middle of the living-room floor, watching as the children settled in for the night, spreading their sleeping bags on the floor or the couch. When the children build forts in the living-room, Maverick would pull on the sheets they'd draped over the dining-room table until the kids shrieked with laughter. When Kearstyn had vivid nightmares and woke up crying, Maverick would rush to her side, licking her face until her sobs turned into laughter as she begged him to stop. Afterwards, he would lay on the couch beside her, a comforting presence in the dark of night.

Above all, Maverick was a good example of perseverance and determination. The kids fed off his attitude. Just watching him enjoy life despite his disability was a powerful lesson to them. If he wouldn't let his struggles stop him, then they wouldn't either. As Kearstyn said, "the best medicine is man's best friend." Especially when that best friend won't let difficulties drag him down.

Maverick has finally slowed down with age. He is a little battle-worn, but he still teaches those with whom he comes into contact not to judge a book by its cover. Though he may have some physical limitations, the sky's the limit when it comes to being a true friend. This wonderful boy is a great ambassador for *Dog's Nation* and a fantastic example of the power of positivity. We could all use a Maverick in our lives, especially on those days when life seems a bit overwhelming.

Chapter Seven
Max

"Before you get a dog, you can't quite imagine what living
with one might be like;
afterward, you can't imagine living any other way."
Caroline Knapp

The scruffy terrier was terrified. The closer I moved, the further he slinked back into the shadows.

"It's okay," I cooed, straining to reach the dog. "I'm not going to hurt you."

A woman named Mrs. Robinson had called to say she'd spotted a black and white terrier mix skulking around the abandoned house next door. "He's awfully skinny," she'd said. "He seems pretty young too."

Glancing out the window, I frowned at the line of black clouds heading my way. "You want me to come out right now? There's a storm brewing and it's growing dark already. Why don't I come out tomorrow morning, instead?"

"But I can hear him whining. He could be hurt."

With a sigh of resignation, I promised her I'd be out within the hour. Which is how I found myself flat on my stomach, in a bed of sodden leaves, scrambling to reach a soggy puppy hiding under the porch steps of a vacant building. As I lay in the dank space, my nose just inches from a large cobweb, I thought longingly of the soft, comfy couch and warm chicken-noodle soup I'd abandoned in order to save a dog who didn't want saving.

"Come on, puppy," I said, scooching further under the sagging steps. A chunk of rotten wood jabbed into my knee. Biting back a cry of pain, I inched forward.

When I'd arrived at the address Mrs. Robinson had provided, I'd discovered an elderly woman waiting on her front porch. The charcoal-black raincoat she was wearing was several sizes too big for her petite and bony frame. Large, winter-green wellington boots reached all the way up to her knees. I briefly wondered if they were her husband's. The bright-pink umbrella she held over her head offered a welcome splash of color on this very dark and dismal evening.

"Mrs. Robinson?"

"The dog is over there," she said without preamble, pointing to a house with boarded up windows and a sagging roof. "He's hiding under the stairs."

My initial plan had been to coax him out with some treats. But the little guy couldn't be lured out. Instead, he huddled deeper into his dark corner.

"Looks like I'm going to have to go in," I said, kneeling in the wet grass. With a grunt, I squeezed under the steps, army-crawling into the dark void beyond. This was certainly not what I'd envisioned when I'd founded *Dog's Nation*. But one thing I'd quickly learned; be prepared for anything, anytime, anywhere.

"You get 'im?" Mrs. Robinson asked, in a loud grating tone of voice.

"Not yet," I replied. "He's pretty scared."

Overhead, the house shivered and groaned in the biting wind. Big, fat drops of rain seeped through every crack in the stairs, the steady drip, drip, drip rendering me soggier by the minute. For just a moment, I considered leaving the dog till the morrow. Maybe by then he'd be hungry and more cooperative. I could even bring someone to help.

I was just picturing my nice, warm bed back home when a pitiful whine broke through my thoughts. The dog's mournful cry spurred me on, reminding me why I was creeping under a decrepit, old house on such a wretched night.

"Come on, boy," I cooed again, stretching my arms as far as I could reach.

His body stiffened and for a second I thought he might lunge.

"You get 'im?" the woman repeated, her face peeking through the gaps in the stairs.

"Not yet, Mrs. Robinson!" I called out. "Come on, buddy. Let's get out of this wet hole and go back to my house where it's nice and warm."

The terrier kept his eyes glued on me, as he shivered in the cold. Raindrops dripped steadily onto his furry little head. He sneezed, then shook his head, sending a spray of water into my eyes. I blinked and swiped at my eyes. This was turning out to be quite an adventure.

Laying there in the cold wet space under the stairs, I struggled to come up with a plan B. I could grab him but wasn't sure whether or not he'd bite. If I'd been thinking properly, I'd have brought a thicker coat and some work gloves to protect my hands.

The sudden noise of a loose shutter slamming against the siding startled the dog, distracting him enough for me to spring forward and come down on top of him. Grabbing him by the scruff of his neck, I pulled him towards me. The dog whimpered as I scooched backwards, out from under the stairs, but didn't put up a fight.

"Get me a towel or something," I told Mrs. Robinson as I cradled the shivering bundle of fur against my chest. "He's wet, filthy, and smells like week-old trash."

The woman hobbled back to her house while I snuggled the quivering puppy against my chest. The frightened terrier was mangy and mud-spattered, but otherwise appeared to be unharmed.

"This is all I have," the elderly woman said, shuffling down the sidewalk with a frayed towel in her hands. "It's not in the best of shape but at least it's clean."

"Thank you."

The woman nodded, patted the dog gently on the head, then watched as I rubbed him down with the towel, then placed him in the dog carrier in the back of my car. "Thanks for calling. I'll check around, see if he belongs to anyone."

"Okay, honey," the old woman said as I handed back the wet towel.

As I drove off, I looked in my rearview mirror. The rain was coming down harder now, but I could still see her bright-pink umbrella bobbing up and down as she shuffled back into her house.

Back home, I took the pup to a vacant pen. As soon as I put him down, he bolted towards the dog house. I set out two bowls, one with water and another with a handful of dry food, then left him to sleep off his grueling escapade.

The next day, I took him to the vet. Though malnourished and flea-ridden, he was in fairly good shape. It was no surprise to discover he wasn't chipped. I contacted the sheriff, the animal shelter, then placed an ad in the paper. No one came forward to claim the little dog. So, I named him Max.

It took a while for Max to overcome some of his fears. At first, he was skittish around people and was terrified of storms. But gradually he discovered he could trust me as well as the helpers who worked at *Dog's Nation*. After several days, he started wagging his tail whenever I or one of my helpers came near his kennel. He stopped being as fearful of the other dogs, eventually coming into my house to sleep on the couch with my own special dogs.

After several weeks, I felt he was ready to train. I took him to the park and the playground where he learned how to walk beside me without straining at the lead. He gradually grew accustomed to the mac trucks driving past as well as the hiss of the breaks when they stopped at the light. He got used to the squeals of laughter coming from kids playing on the swings and stopped shying away from anyone who approached him. He learned what was expected of him at church, at the store, and other public places.

Next, we worked on riding the elevator and going up and down grate stairs. He took it all in stride as if he'd been doing it all his life. Max was turning out to be a fine service dog.

Max had been with me for several months when I received a call from an acquaintance. A friend of hers had a daughter, Amber, who was on the autism spectrum. Even though Amber attended a private school for children with special needs, she still struggled quite a bit. She was experiencing a great deal of digestive issues and some mornings she was so sick to her stomach; she couldn't go to school. Her mom would have to take the day off work and worried she might lose her job. When Amber did make it to school, she was often agitated, spiraling into severe meltdowns. As her anxiety continued to peak, her grades continued to plunge. My friend wondered whether I might have a smaller dog that could help Amber. I immediately thought of Max.

When I introduced the two, it was love at first sight. Max liked this vibrant, cheerful girl and Amber was immediately enamored with the playful terrier. And so began Max's intense training. He learned how to board a school bus and how to sit quietly beside his girl. He learned what was expected of him while at school and how to mind his girl when she was on the playground without getting distracted by the other children. Once Max successfully completed his training and all the certifications and paperwork were completed, the little terrier moved to his forever home.

A couple of weeks later, Amber's mother called me. She was bubbling with excitement. She informed me that Amber loved her dog, and the two of them did everything together.

"My daughter loves to swing but didn't like the fact that Max couldn't be with her on the swing. So, she snuggles him on her lap while she swings. Every night, Max snuggles with her in bed, alleviating her fear of the dark. He even worked a booth with her when she sold cookies at the Dragonfest school fund-raiser."

When Amber had to go undergo a medical procedure, Max was there with her the whole time, his reassuring presence easing some of her fear and accelerating the healing process. He also travelled with Amber and her mom when they took a tour of Nasa, relieving some of the anxiety she experiences when travelling.

"That dog has done more for our little girl than I'd ever thought possible," her mother said. "Not only is she happy and more confident at school, but her grades have improved considerably. Max has drawn her out of her melancholy and given her more confidence."

I'm so glad I didn't give up on him that wet, stormy day. Because I persisted, Max and his girl have both discovered that life is a little easier when we have someone to walk alongside us.

Chapter Eight
Hickman

"Saving one dog will not change the world,
But surely for that one dog, the world will change forever."
Author Unknown

"Shawn, this is Betty, from the vet clinic in Nevada." Her voice sounded strained.

"Hi, Betty. What's up?"

"We had a pit bull-lab-mix come in to be euthanized –."

"What's wrong with it?"

"Nothing. That's the whole problem. He's a beautiful dog with a vibrant personality. When the shelter brought him in, he was wagging his tail, and I could swear he was smiling at us." Betty's voice broke.

"How old is he?" I asked, mainly just to give her time to collect herself.

"He's still a pup, really. Large paws, big ears, broad head, and an energetic temperament. He has so much charisma and personality, we just couldn't go through with it. I'd take him, but I already have two dogs. You know we don't normally do this, but we all want to give this dog another chance. Would there be any way you could take him?"

"Of course." There was no hesitation on my part. Savings lives and serving those in need are *Dog's Nation* top priorities. "I can probably make it out there later today, if you can hold him till then."

"We'd love to. Thank you, Shawn." She sounded so relieved it brought a smile to my face.

Betty was spot on. The pit bull-lab mix was everything she had mentioned, and more. As soon as Betty let him out of his kennel, the dog rushed up to me as if I were his long-lost friend. He was a formidable dog, at least fifty to sixty pounds of brawn and energy. His tail was constantly in motion, and his tongue hung out one side of his mouth in a cute and quirky manner. His fur was as dark and smooth as ebony and his large, adoring eyes were the color of hot Mocha, flecked with golden sunlight. They reeled me, hook, line, and sinker. I was in love.

"We're all so relieved you're taking this guy home," Betty said. "He has too much love and joy-de-vivre to be put down."

"Exactly," I said, snapping on a lead. "I'm so glad you called me. He will make a wonderful service dog. You ready to go home, buddy?"

The dog looked at me, head tilted sideways as though eager to understand what I was saying. He would be easy to train.

"Come on, then." I opened the front door and he trotted happily after me, hopped into the cargo area in the back of my car, then laid down as though knowing he was in good company.

The volunteers at *Dog's Nation* were instantly enamored. He had a vitality and enthusiasm about life that was contagious. He didn't simply walk, he trotted. He didn't simply eat, he slurped and savored. He didn't simply wag his tail; he shook his entire body like a tractor revving up its engine.

It was one of *Dog's Nation*'s volunteers who asked if her dad could name him. We typically like to extend the honor of naming our rescue dogs to our local veterans. So, Floyd Jimenez stopped by one day and met our newest four-legged trainee.

Chief Warrant Officer Jimenez served as a helicopter pilot during the Vietnam War. Although he had many narrow escapes, none compared to the day he was assigned the simple mission of flying a General to another base.

As Officer Jimenez headed out to begin the pre-flight check onboard his Huey, a staff sergeant called him into his office.

"Change of plans, Officer Jimenez. I know it's last minute, but I just received orders to send you to SERE training. You'll be leaving in thirty minutes."

SERE is a U.S. military program that trains military personnel in survival, evasion, resistance, and escape.

"What about my mission, Sir? I was assigned to fly General Johnston out, Sir."

"Another Chief Warrant Officer will take that flight. Go pack your bags."

"Sir, yes, Sir."

Although Officer Jimenez was surprised by this sudden change in plans, he didn't think much of it until he returned ten days later and learned the officer who had been assigned to fly General Johnston out was killed by hostile fire. The Huey crashed and everyone on board perished that day.

Floyd Jimenez was severely shaken by this news and asked the name of the officer who had flown the Huey that fateful night. His name was David Allen Hickman, of Okaloosa County, Florida. Officer Jimenez never forgot the man who died in his stead. So, when he came to *Dog's Nation* and learned we were training our newest member to be a service dog, he asked if we could name him Hickman. We were honored to name this tremendous service dog after one of America's finest heroes. Later, Officer

Jimenez brought us this poem he wrote in honor of the brave pilot who took his place.

Why

I never really knew him
I can't recall his name
I only know since that day
I've never been the same.

We were on a routine flight
We flew some VIP
They sent him out to meet us
He traded places with me.

They sent me to survival school
Why I'll never know
The only choice they gave me
Was to pack a bag and go.

When I returned ten days later
I learned that he had died
No one ever saw the tears
But deep inside I cried.

I guess someday I will learn
The reason as to why
On that day God chose him
Instead of me to die.

Floyd W. Jimenez
CW3 USAR, Retired

Dedicated to the memory of
CW2 David Allen Hickman
Born August 11, 1946
Killed in Action, December 4, 1969
In South Vietnam, Binh Thuy province
Served with 1st Aviation Brigade,
68th Aviation Company

Chapter Nine
Amy

"I now have a dog that I care for,
I see things that I needed to see.
That lovely dog that I rescued,
really ended up rescuing me."
Author Unknown

I usually avoid the term 'rescued' for it implies I do the saving, when most of the time it's the other way around. Amy was a perfect example of this.

I'd received a call from a nearby shelter, informing me they had a female terrier-mix that was scheduled to be euthanized the following day.

"Let me come over and take a peek at her," I told the coordinator.

That's how I found myself in a back room of the animal shelter, staring into a pair of soft, doleful brown eyes.

"Hello, Amy," I said, crouching to get a better look at her. The look in a dog's eyes speaks volumes about its temperament.

Head cocked to one side; the terrier-mix peered through the bars. "Arf!" she said, her tail sweeping the concrete floor. Her black, wiry coat sported a tiny splash of white on the chest. She was attentive, listening to every word I said, her short ears erect, her dark brown eyes alert.

"Amy is extremely friendly and very well-behaved," the shelter coordinator said. "Seems such a shame to put her down simply because no one has adopted her and she's run out of time."

I nodded. Unfortunately, this happens all too often. "Would you like to come home with me?"

The little terrier rose up on her short legs, her tail whipping back and forth like windshield wipers in a downpour.

"I'll adopt her," I said, determined to save this sweet little gal.

Amy quickly proved just how clever she was, responding when I called her and obeying simple commands such as 'sit' and 'stay.' In no time, she'd mastered basic directives such as walking properly on the lead without giving in to distractions. It seemed a shame that such an intelligent dog had never found her forever home.

Within a month, Amy graduated to walks in public venues where she learned to stay focused on her tasks. I trained her how to stop and block at pedestrian crosswalks, the proper way to conduct herself around people and other animals. She was astute and eager to learn, her keen mind quickly grasping what I required of her.

Amy had been with me for several months and was progressing nicely when I received a call from a couple with a non-verbal twelve-year old son on the spectrum.

"My wife and I haven't slept properly for years," the man said. "Because Jacob will leave the house on his own, my wife and I have to watch him twenty-four, seven. We can't leave him unattended for even a few seconds. Our other kids help out when they can, but we are at our wits' end."

I could hear the fatigue and desperation in his voice. "When can you come over?" I asked, my mind running through the dogs I was training, that might potentially be a good match for this young boy. "I need to assess your son's needs, pair him up with the best dog for his unique requirements, then spend a few days training together."

He let out an audible sigh of frustration. "We can't do that."

"It's important for you to know the commands and signals I've taught your service dog in order for her to assist your son properly," I said. It is critical that each potential handler participate in the training process in order to bond with their service dog and learn the behaviors, commands, and tasks their service dog has mastered.

"We live two and a half hours away," he said, "and my employer won't let me take more than one day off right now. We're haying and it's all hands on deck until winter when things slow down a bit."

I was dumbfounded. "Where do you work?"

"I work on a ranch. My boss has been kind enough to offer us free housing on the property but it comes at a price."

My brain started churning, trying to come up with some options. Ideally, I liked to spend a few days with the family that received the service dog so I could teach them everything they needed to know about the dog's skills and training.

"Do you have some time right now to go through your son's history so I can work with the dog I have in mind? I want to make sure she's properly trained to meet your son's need and keep him safe. I'll also need you to provide me with a note from your son's physician stating his need for a service dog."

After discussing Jacob's particular case over the phone, I had a better idea what he required in a service dog. I would pair him with Amy, which meant I needed to teach her how to anchor him when the family was out in public, how to alert the parents if he decided to run off on his own, how to de-escalate an autism meltdown, and distract him before his anxiety peaked.

After several weeks of intensive training, Jacob's family came to pick up Amy. By then, I was confident in her ability to take on her new responsibility; Jacob. I had filled a notebook with instructions so his parents would know everything she was trained to do, the commands I had taught her, and reminders on how to care for their service dog.

I was on my third cup of coffee on that cold, blustery day when I heard the crunch of tires on gravel. Out the kitchen window, I saw a van edging up my drive, kicking up a thick cloud of dust in its wake. A chorus of barks broke out in the kennels out back, while in the pasture, Angel stomped her foot and nickered.

Gulping down a last swig of coffee, I opened the door and stepped out onto the porch. A tall man in work overalls emerged from the van. With one hand, he shoved his large-brimmed, woven sea grass hat atop his head, then slammed the driver's door closed with the other. His windburned face and furrowed brow testified to hours of work in the fields.

"Mornin'" he said, tipping his hat. "I'm lookin' for Miz Abell."

I nodded. "That's me."

"My name's Eli. Nice to meet you. I see you have quite the greetin' committee."

I chuckled. "Yes, they're better than any doorbell."

"We sure do 'preciate what you're doing for our boy."

"You're quite welcome."

"This is my wife, Sarah," he said, as she climbed from the van and walked over to join us. She was a striking woman with gentle eyes, delicate features, and hair the color of golden wheat.

"Pleased to meet you," she said, reaching out to shake my hand.

I was about to respond when the van's door slid open, disgorging a steady stream of kids. I counted eight.

"Come on out, Jacob," his father said, thrusting his upper half into the van.

For a second, I wondered how Amy would do with so many children. Why hadn't they told me they had nine kids when I talked to them on the phone? Then again, Amy had plenty of experience with noise and crowds. She could take care of herself and Jacob as well.

A young boy stepped hesitantly from the van. Head lowered, he stood next to the door, the fingertips on his right hand tapping his thigh at a steady rhythm.

"Jacob," his father called out. "Come meet Shawn."

Jacob continued to drum his fingers against his leg, staring at nothing in particular.

"Remember I talked about Shawn yesterday? She's going to help us," his father persisted.

A flicker of the eyes in my direction was all the reaction his father's words produced.

"Let me fetch the dog," I said, startled when Jacob stooped, plucked a blade of grass, then shoved it in his mouth. Neither one of his parents seemed surprised by this unusual behavior.

Several minutes later, I returned with the little terrier. Like the sun breaking through the clouds, Jacob's face lit up at the sight of Amy.

"Jacob, this is Amy," I said, leading her towards him. "Would you like to come say hello to her?"

Jacob seemed hesitant, as though he were afraid of the dog. Crouching next to Amy, I stroked her head. "See, she likes to be petted. Want to try?"

Slowly, carefully, Jacob stepped forward, hand outstretched.

"It's okay, Jacob. She won't hurt you."

Though he didn't speak, I could tell Jacob understood everything I was saying. Cautious, Jacob crouched down beside me.

"See, her tail is wagging," I said, one eye on the boy, the other on the dog. "That means she likes you and wants to play with you."

Gently, Jacob reached out and laid a hand on Amy's head.

"Aarf," she barked. Startled, Jacob whipped his hand away and toppled backwards, landing on his rump.

We all watched with bated breath to see how Jacob would respond. Instead of the anticipated meltdown, a squeal of laughter burst from his lips, a beautiful, musical sound that lit up his parents' faces.

"This is the first time we've heard him laugh," his mother said softly, tears brimming in her eyes.

Amy licked Jacobs' chin. His eyes grew wide as he looked at the dog then turned to look at me.

"That's her way of saying she likes you. You can give her a hug if you like her too."

Immediately, the boy wrapped his arms around the terrier. Beside me, Jacob's mother gasped and raised a hand to her mouth. "He pulls away from me whenever I touch him, but here he is, hugging a dog."

"That's often the case for individuals with autism," I told her, smiling as I watched Amy dart away, then run circles around him, tail wagging with excitement.

"Try tossing this to her," I said, handing the boy a yellow tennis ball.

Curious, the boy took the ball, then dropped it on the ground. Immediately, the dog ran over, picked it up in her jaws and ran off with it.

"You have to throw it, like this," I said, fetching another ball, then flinging it across the yard. The terrier took off like a racehorse out of the gate. She snatched up the ball and returned to me, the tennis ball clenched firmly between her teeth.

"Drop the ball," I commanded. Amy obediently opened her mouth and let it plop down at my feet.

"Good girl," I said, petting her.

"Now you try." Handing the ball to Jacob, I watched as he cocked his arm and let the ball fly.

"Wow! You've got a strong throwing arm!"

The boy glanced up at me and offered a hesitant smile. But it was enough for me to know he would be okay.

After teaching his parents all the signals and behaviors I'd taught Amy and all the necessary paperwork and arrangements were done, I sent them on their way; two parents with a renewed sense of hope, eight excited children, one little boy with much promise, and a sweet little terrier who had finally found her forever home.

Several weeks later, I received a phone call from Jacob's father. "My wife and I wanted to let you know Amy is one of our greatest blessings. She has worked wonders with our boy."

"That's wonderful!" I said, delighted to hear from them.

"Since the day Amy came home with us, Jacob has changed for the better. For one thing, he now sleeps in his own bed, Amy curled up beside him. The two of them are inseparable. Amy follows Jacob everywhere and we often find the two of them playing fetch with the tennis ball you gave us. In fact, the other day, we heard Jacob speak his first words; "Run, Amy, run."

A tear trickled down my cheek as I heard the excitement in Eli's voice. At last, their son had found his voice.

"How special that must have been for you." My voice was thick with emotion.

"Sarah and I cried tears of joy. But wait, there's more. Yesterday, my wife heard Amy scratching at the door. She was barking and carrying on in such a frantic manner that Sarah knew something was terribly wrong. She ran outside and immediately, Amy took off. Realizing the dog would never leave Jacob alone unless he was in danger, Sarah followed her, through the cow pasture and down to the pond where she found Jacob waist-deep in the water. Our son doesn't know how to swim."

Eli's voice was husky with emotion.

"I'm so glad he's okay," I replied, softly. I was about to cry too. "Thanks for telling me."

The little terrier I'd saved from certain death had saved his boy from drowning. Miracles like this are the reason I founded *Dog's Nation*. Many times, when we rescue a dog and train them as a service dog, we don't just save one life, we save two.

Chapter Ten
Battle Buddy Tillman

"Friends come and go...
Battle Buddies last forever."
Author Unknown

"Shawn? This is Roy Anderson."

I let out a sigh. When the police chief calls, it's usually because he wants me to help him out. "Hello, Roy. What do you have for me this time?"

Roy chuckled. "What? Can't I simply call to say hello?"

"When was the last time you called me just to chat?" I countered.

"Okay, you're right." He sucked in a deep breath. "A few weeks ago, animal control found two dogs running along highway 54. Neither one had tags or chips."

"Of course not," I answered, pinching the bridge of my nose.

"One of them is a pit bull, about one year old. I know you..."

"… take in pit bulls," I finished for him. "What breed is the other dog?"

"It looks a bit like a terrier, but I think it's a mixture of several breeds. The pit bull actually belongs to a Bobby Barrett; I think you know him?"

"Yeah, he's helped us walk the dogs a few times. He and his elderly mother live in a trailer on the south end of town."

"He says he can't afford the penalty fees to get his dog out of the pound. Apparently, Bobby's mom has been diagnosed with brain cancer and every penny goes towards medical bills. I'm hoping you could take the dogs as they'll be euthanized tomorrow if no one adopts them."

Though he tries to put on an air of indifference, our city's chief of police is a softy when it comes to animals. He'll do practically anything to save a healthy dog or cat from being euthanized. Of course, he knew I would too.

"Of course, I'll take them. Tell the pound I'll be around to pick them up as soon as I can. It might not be until tomorrow, though. I've got three dogs in training and I'm expecting my helpers any moment now."

"Right-oh." Without even so much as a thank-you or a goodbye, Roy hung up. I could visualize him sitting behind his large metal desk stacked high with pending files, fist-pumping in victory.

It wasn't until the next afternoon that I was able to collect the dogs.

"We're so glad you're taking them, Shawn," the shelter coordinator said. "They are both such cuties!"

I watched her amble down the hall, a loud ruckus welling up as she entered the kennel area; they had a full house. It makes me sick to think how many smart, wonderful dogs are euthanized, simply because they 'ran out of time.' Dogs who could assist veterans to live happy, productive lives. Dogs who could be trained to ease autistic meltdowns or prevent drownings in individuals with autism. Dogs who want nothing more than to love and be loved.

Soon, the coordinator returned, escorting two sweet bundles of cuteness. Like a little child released from school, the pit bull mix rushed past her, bounding down the hall, tongue lolling, a goofy grin on his adorable face. His coat was mostly tan with a renegade streak of white that started in the middle of his broad head, trickling down between his eyes and around his snout. Rushing up to me, the puppy ran circles around my legs, skidding on the newly-mopped floors.

"He likes you," the coordinator said, laughing. On her heels came a small dog, most likely a terrier mix. She appeared a bit more contained and wary, although she wagged her tail when she saw me. The tips of her ears quivered in anticipation as if she knew she was going somewhere delightful.

Crouching, I stroked her on the head. Immediately, the pit bull nosed his way between us, eager for some attention.

"Yes, I know. You want some loving too," I say, as I scratched him between the ears. The pup leaned into me and swept the floor with his tail.

"You two ready to go explore your new digs?" The swift wagging of their tails was answer enough.

After putting a collar on each of the dogs, I snapped on their leads and led them out to my car. Opening the back hatch, I patted the floor of the cargo area. "Come on, then. Let's go home."

Apparently, they knew that word for they both jumped into the back. Nose to the floor, they sniffed every inch of the cargo area.

"Will that do okay for you two?" I said, chuckling.

The pit bull gazed at me; head tilted to one side as if trying to measure my words. With a loud moan, he laid down on all fours, then rested his head on his front paws. I threw back my head and laughed.

"Really?" I slammed the hatch closed, then slid into the driver seat. It felt good to laugh again. It had been way too long.

I wasn't too sure how either of them would do in the car. Some dogs love it, others get anxious and won't stay in their designated spot. If needed, I could contain them in dog crates, but these two had been in cages so long that I was reluctant to confine them once more. Fortunately, they were good as gold. Every once in a while, I'd hear a slight groan or see a black nose poking over the back of the rear seats, but otherwise it was a fairly uneventful trip home.

As I pulled into the driveway, my heart skipped a beat. My son's pickup truck was parked in front of the house. He was about to be deployed overseas to serve as a front-line Joint Terminal Attack Controller (JTAC).

"Hey, Mom!" he said, stepping off the porch as I climbed from the car. "Thought I'd stop by and say good-bye before I take off."

Even though I'd suspected as much, the news hit me like a punch in the chest. For a second, I couldn't breathe. Even though this wasn't his first deployment, it still filled me with fear and apprehension. I reached up and held his face in my hands. "When do you fly out?"

"Tomorrow. Early."

"I sure hope this is the last time you deploy," I said, tears welling in my eyes. "Be safe."

"Always, Mom. Always." He bent to kiss me on the forehead, then wiped the tear that trickled down my cheek. "Don't cry, Mom. I'll be okay. I promise."

Shaking my head to clear away the painful thoughts, I smiled up at him. "Want to meet my new recruits?"

"Absolutely, Sergeant Major!" he said, clicking his heels together as he saluted.

As soon as I opened the hatch, William's face broke into a huge grin. "They're both beautiful dogs, mom, but this pit bull is magnificent."

"Keep an eye on them, while I fill the water bowls," I said, patting his arm.

When I came back out, I discovered William was playing fetch with the dogs. Jaws clenched around a yellow tennis ball, the pit bull raced about, dodging William's playful tackles. A bittersweet smile played at the corners of my mouth as I stored this special moment in my memory.

Wearily, I sat down on the top step and sighed. The three of them had more energy than I could ever muster. Good thing I had a group of volunteers to help me exercise the dogs.

William ended up naming the dogs. The terrier he called Millie and the pit bull Tillman, after Patrick

Daniel Tillman, the American football player who left his sports career to enlist in the US Army in the aftermath of the September 11th attacks. Tillman was also the name for the Battle Buddy Program.

William's departure to parts unknown left a big void. I constantly worried about his safety and that worry often provoke anxiety attacks, especially when I heard about unrest in the Middle East. My heart and chest ached, as though something or someone was sucking the air out of me. I had very vivid dreams about William in the thick of combat, waking up with tears coursing down my cheeks.

Tillman could sense my wavering moods, especially when I was worried or distressed. He would lay beside me on the bed or the couch, licking my face and nudging me persistently with his wet nose until I stopped crying. His presence was a distraction, helping slow my heart rate and reduce my stress. His love and devotion were the best remedy for my anxiety. Tillman became my battle buddy, a gift from God to help me through this difficult time.

Tillman was trained to be an ambassador for *Dog's Nation* while Millie was eventually adopted out to a family with a little girl who had just lost her own dog. One of my friends sewed an army vest for Tillman with tags identical to Pat Tillman's, that read, 'U.S. Army' on one side and 'Tillman' on the other.

His vest even had a dog tag clipped to one of the buckles. "Tillman," I said, fastening it around his back and chest," you are now officially my battle buddy."

One of the volunteers at *Dog's Nation* was a boy named C.J. He and his mom and three sisters were temporarily living at a shelter for victims of domestic violence. Training the dogs afforded all of them an opportunity to get out and do something helpful for their community. The children loved the time they spent with the dogs, walking them and teaching them new skills. In many ways, it was therapeutic for the kids as well as their parent. There's nothing like a dog to lift your spirits.

For some reason, C.J. and Tillman took an instant liking to each other. C.J. was savvy with dogs, as though training them were second-nature to him. Under my supervision, C.J. walked Tillman around the park on the lead, trained him how to go up and down grate-type stairs, took him on the elevator, and walked him around the rubberized track in the community center. They both accompanied me to the Little House Children's Theatre where C.J. was learning how to perform plays in front of audiences. Tillman would lay on the floor, lending a listening ear to children practicing their lines, or substitute as a pillow to tired kids waiting for their cue.

C.J.'s father was eventually released from prison, having served his jailtime. Ten days later, he died from a freak accident. When I heard the news, I knew Tillman and I needed to attend the funeral, if nothing else than to offer support.

The day of the funeral dawned grey and overcast, suitable for such a melancholy day. The service was held in a small, nondescript chapel nestled among ancient headstones, weather-beaten and long forgotten. I pushed through the heavy wooden doors and into the hushed stillness of the chapel. A handful of people occupied the first row, speaking in hushed voices. C.J. must have heard the click of Hillman's claws against the cold stone floor for he whipped around, then jumped up and hurried down the aisle, dropping to his knees as he threw his arms around Tillman and sobbed into the dog's neck. The dog never flinched, but stood fast, the best solace a grieving child could ever know.

Crouching beside C.J., I placed a hand on the boy's head then thrust the leash into his hand. "Why don't you take Tillman to sit with you during the service?" I whispered.

C.J. lifted his head to look at me and nodded. Leading the dog to the front pew, C.J. patted the wood bench. Tillman jumped up, then leaned into C.J. when he sat down. Like a true battle buddy,

Tillman sat beside C.J. throughout the entire service, showing himself a true friend in the midst of C.J.'s grief.

Several weeks after the funeral, I received a call from Bobby. The sheriff had informed him I'd adopted his dog. "Thank you for saving my dog," he said, his voice shaky with emotion. "Ma has been battling cancer for a while. She has a brain tumor. She'd come home and leave the door open behind her, so the dog kept getting out. I just couldn't afford those penalty fees each time I had to fetch him from the pound."

"I heard about your mom. I'm so sorry, Bobby."

"She's real confused now. Lives at Bellevue nursing home. She thinks she's still at home and keeps asking me to let the dog in."

"If you give me the nursing home address, I'd be glad to pay her a visit and bring Tillman along. She might be glad to see him again."

"She sure would like that," Bobby said. "Thank you, Miss Shawn."

The very next day, I took Tillman to visit Rita Barrett. She looked so frail and gaunt laying in her bed.

"Hello, Mrs. Barrett," I said, leaning close so she could see and hear me. "I brought you a visitor."

Rita seemed to recognize me and struggled to sit up in bed.

"You don't have to get up, Mrs. Barrett. I'll bring Tillman to you."

I lifted Tillman onto the bed next to Mrs. Barrett. Raising a thin, bony hand, she placed it on Tillman's head. The dog laid down beside her, resting his head on her chest. Even though he hadn't seen her in quite a while, he obviously hadn't forgotten her.

"His name is Tillman now, Mrs. Barrett. Battle Buddy Tillman. He's happy to see you again."

She offered a feeble smile, then mumbled something I couldn't quite understand. But I could tell she was happy we'd come to see her. I gently touched her hand and promised to bring Tillman back for another visit.

Paying a visit to Mrs. Barrett became one of our weekly activities. Every Tuesday afternoon at 2 p.m., Tillman would wait by the front door for our ride to the nursing home. But Rita was not the only one who enjoyed these visits. Tillman quickly developed quite a cluster of fans at Bellevue. As soon as we'd walk through the nursing home doors, residents and staff would gather around us, barely acknowledging me as they fussed and fawned over 'their beautiful boy.'

One day, a nurse pulled me aside. "Mrs. Barrett was quite lucid for a short while last night."

I looked at her in surprise. So far, Mrs. Barrett's mumblings hadn't made much sense to me.

"That sometimes happens before they pass. People perk up, become more clear-minded, and even appear to improve right before their bodies shut down. It's a strange phenomenon. Anyway, she requested Tillman be with her when she passes."

"We would be honored to be there," I said, providing her with my cell phone number.

Two days later I received a call from Bellevue, around one in the morning. Mrs. Barrett hadn't long to live. I half expected it because Tillman had been behaving strangely all evening and into the night, pacing and whining as though something were bothering him.

When we arrived at the nursing home, the family had already gathered to say their goodbyes. Tillman went straight to Rita's bed and pawed at the covers. Lifting the dog onto the bed, I placed him beside her. Mrs. Barrett's eyes flickered open, a feeble hand lifted off the bedsheet, struggling to touch Tillman. Gently, I lifted her small hand and laid it on Tillman's head. The faintest of smiles played on her lips. Minutes later, she took in a final breath then slipped away.

The following Tuesday, Tillman headed for the door at 2 p.m. as usual.

"Mrs. Barrett isn't at Bellevue anymore," I told Tillman. I was a little perplexed for usually dogs understand death. But Tillman wouldn't be deterred. It was Tuesday afternoon and he wanted to go to Bellevue. When we got to the nursing home, I fully expected Tillman to head straight for Rita's old room. Instead, he strode into one room after another, visiting with the other residents whom he had befriended during his previous visits. Tillman understood what I had failed to grasp; there was still work to do at Bellevue, even though Rita was gone.

The cold winter finally surrendered to a beautiful spring. I looked forward to seeing William soon. He would be coming home for a short leave of absence and I was counting the days. Just as I was beginning to experience a sense of relief, my world was turned upside down by a phone call.

My oldest son, Shane, had suffered a seizure and had been taken by ambulance to a hospital in Springfield. Snatching my purse off the dining-room table along with my keys, I grabbed the dog lead and snapped it on Tillman's collar. After checking in with the volunteers who assured me they would take care of the other dogs, I drove off with Tillman riding shot-gun. I needed my battle buddy's support now, more than ever.

The hospital in Springfield was several blocks long. Parking in the nearest spot I could find, I hurried into the building with Tillman at my side. The harsh smell of Clorox and bleach hit me as soon as I walked through the sliding double doors. To this day, the smell of Clorox resuscitates memories from that terrible day.

In the main lobby, a receptionist directed me to a bank of elevators to the right of her desk. "Those elevators will take you right to the Intensive Care Unit."

I thanked her, then called the elevator. Heart pounding like a kettle-drum, I waited for it to arrive. It seemed to take an eternity. When the shiny grey doors finally slid open, a woman stepped off, face downcast, her eyes red and swollen. As I stepped onto the elevator, I sucked in a deep breath, trying to calm the dread that was building up inside of me. Yet the confined space, the humming and groaning of the cables as they carried me upward only served to exacerbate the hammering inside my chest.

Finally, the elevator stopped, the welcome ping alerting me that we'd reached ICU. Stepping off the elevator, I was immediately sucked into an atmosphere of subdued expectancy. Hushed conversations, muted beeps from life-saving monitors, dim lights, and muffled sobs all contributed to the palpable tension in the family waiting area. ICU is a place where souls are suspended between life and death. A place where each breath is treasured and futures can turn on a dime.

Walking through the sliding glass doors with "Intensive Care Unit" painted in bold, capital letters, I noticed twelve patient rooms set in a circle around the nurses' station. Several crash carts stood at the ready, a stark reminder that none of us is promised tomorrow.

At the desk, a woman in blue scrubs looked up from her computer. "May I help you?"

"I am Shane Abell's mother."

"Ah, yes. He's down in Imaging right now, having an MRI. If you'd be so kind to have a seat in the waiting area, I'll let his nurse know you're here."

Nodding, I retraced my steps back to the cluster of chairs in the small, cramped room designated for families and visitors. A young couple huddled together in one corner, holding hands, their heads bowed as they prayed quietly. On the other side of the room an older man sat hunched over, alone in his grief, his weathered face streaked with tears. His grizzled hair was mussed up, as though he'd run his hands through it over and over.

Sinking into one of the grey twill barrel chairs, I closed my eyes and let out a sigh. I felt Tillman lean against my legs, a reassuring presence in my time of need. Leaning forward, I wrapped my arms around my battle buddy, burying my face in his soft fur as I prayed silently for my son.

"That your dog?"

I glanced up. The older gentleman was staring at Tillman. I nodded.

"What's his name?"

"Tillman. My son named him after Pat Tillman," I offered.

"He reminds me of my dog, Sally. She was my best friend when I came home from Vietnam. Don't know if I'd still be here if she hadn't helped me through some of the darkest days of my life. Sure could use her company about now."

I nodded. There was no need for words.

"Mind if I pet him?" the man asked.

Looking into his eyes, I saw raw pain and despair. I don't typically allow strangers to pet my dogs when they're wearing their work vests because they're 'on the job.' But this man needed what only Tillman could give; unconditional love and support.

"Sure," I say, leading Tillman over to him.

The amazing thing about dogs is their intuitive understanding of people's feelings. Leaning against the man's legs, Tillman offered him a look that seemed to say, "Go ahead, hug me if that will help."

The elderly man leaned down, gently wrapped his arms around Tillman, and began to sob. Tillman didn't budge, just leaned into him all the more, offering the grieving man a shoulder to cry on. Most of the time, that's infinitely more helpful than words.

"Sorry," the man said, swiping at his tears.

Reaching for the box of Kleenex on the coffee table, I handed it to him. He wiped his eyes, blew his nose, then cleared his throat. "My wife was in a car accident."

"I'm sorry to hear that," I offered.

"You have family in there?" he asked, pointing to the ICU doors.

"My son."

We lapsed into silence, two hurting souls fearing the worst but hoping for the best. Tillman laid down, his head resting on his front paws. His eyes flickered back and forth between the man and me, watching, waiting.

After what seemed like a very long time, a doctor stepped into the waiting room. The stitching over the pocket on his lab coat informed me I was dealing with Dr. Huffman. "Mrs. Abell?"

I popped out of my seat. "Yes?"

"Your son is back from MRI. You may come and see him for a few minutes, but we want to keep the visit brief. He's sedated, so he may not respond to you. If you'd like to follow me?"

I nodded to the elderly man. "I hope your wife is okay," I said, then turned to follow the doctor.

"Will Shane be alright?" I asked, as we stepped through the door separating the waiting room from the ICU ward.

"He had what we call a status seizure. It was severe enough that he coded in the ambulance on the way here."

I sucked in a deep breath, shocked at the news.

"He's stable now, but we are still working on the cause. Does he have epilepsy, or a history of seizures?" Dr. Huffman asked, pausing in front of Shane's room.

I shook my head. "No, in fact, I don't think there's even a family history of seizures."

"We'll do a full workup on him and see if we can find the trigger. In the meantime, why don't you go on in and sit with your son?"

Tears welled in my eyes as I looked upon my son laying so still in that hospital bed. Padded covers had been placed between the mattress and the rails to prevent injury should he seize again. An IV had been inserted into the back of his hand and machines recorded his heartbeat, pulse rate, and oxygen levels.

Clasping his clammy hand in mine, I whispered his name. "Shane." There was no response. "Shane, this is mom. And Tillman. He's right here, next to your bed."

Taking his hand, I slid it between the rails and placed it on Tillman's head. "He's rooting for you, and so am I." I thought I glimpsed a flicker of movement in the hand resting atop the dog's head, then again that could have been wishful thinking.

After several minutes of quiet prayer, Tillman and I headed home. As we passed one of the other rooms, I caught sight of the man from the waiting room, holding his wife's hand. Her head was bandaged and one leg was in a cast, but she was awake and talking. They would be okay.

Back home, I sank onto the couch. I suddenly realized how exhausted I was. A deep sadness and weariness pulled at my soul. Both of my sons were in a battle, struggling for survival. Laying my head against the back of the couch, I closed my eyes and let out a deep sigh. Without hesitation, Tillman climbed onto the sofa and laid with his head in my lap, his way of offering empathy.

"Thank you, Tillman," I whispered, stroking his head. I laid my head back on the couch. Within seconds, I was fast asleep.

The next few days were full with daily visits to Shane in the ICU. At times, he seemed to be doing better, then he'd suffer another seizure and regress back to square one. As a result, Tillman and I spent many hours in the Intensive Care waiting room, popping into Shane's room every couple hours for a brief visit, then returning to the waiting room to offer comfort to grieving family members. Within days, Tillman was known around the hospital as "that sweet dog in the ICU." He grew so popular that medical staff would stop by the ICU waiting room to say hi and pat him on the head.

One day, as we stepped off the elevator, Tillman and I were met by a couple of nurses. "What happened to Shane?" I asked, fearing the worst.

"Shane is fine, Mrs. Abell," one of the nurses said, her face breaking into a big smile. "But we do want to show you something. Come see."

Startled, I followed her into the ICU waiting room. In the far corner was a fleece-covered dog bed. "This is Tillman's for as long as your son stays in the hospital. We thought he deserved it after helping so many people. Even the chaplain is thinking he might get a therapy dog just to make his job here a little easier," she laughed.

I was touched beyond words. Just to know how much Tillman was loved and appreciated, validated my vision at *Dog's Nation*. Witnessing first-hand what Tillman had to offer just by being there to comfort and help those who were grieving was well worth all the time and effort I put into this endeavor. He was so cherished by visitors and hospital staff alike that if someone commented about 'the pit bull,' they were quickly corrected with the simple statement, "No, that's Tillman."

When Shane was finally discharged from the hospital, his departure was met with tears. While they were glad my son had recovered and was going home, they would miss Tillman. I had to promise we would return occasionally just to visit.

With Shane out of the hospital and William due to come home soon, life finally started to settle down again. I resumed my responsibilities at *Dog's Nation*, spending most of my time training and matching the dogs with clients requesting a service dog.

C.J. and I were walking the dogs around the track in the community center one day when he blurted out "I'm scared, Miss Shawn."

"What are you afraid of?"

"I got a lump right here." He turned his head so I could see the bulge on the left side of his neck. "One of the nurses at the shelter noticed it and she made an appointment for me to see Dr. Brown."

C.J. tried to put on a brave front, but I could tell he was extremely nervous. "I'm afraid he's gonna have to operate on it."

"You know Dr. Brown is a very good doctor, don't you?"

C.J. glanced up at me, then quickly lowered his gaze so I wouldn't see the tears brimming in his eyes.

"Would you like Tillman to go with you? I can check with the clinic and see if that's okay with them."

A timid smile appeared. "Could he, Miss Shawn? That would be awesome!"

"I'll have to get the doctor's okay, first. But I don't see why not."

Doctor Brown was more than happy to have Tillman escort C.J. to his office. And so, we sat in the exam room while the doctor lanced the cyst. C.J. pressed his face into the dog's shoulder while the physician cleaned and numbed the site, Tillman nuzzling C.J.'s hand as though trying to distract him. Within minutes, the cyst was lanced and drained.

"It appears to be an infection that should clear up with antibiotics," Dr. Brown stated. "Well done, C.J.! And Tillman," he added.

That entire experience strengthened the bond between C.J. and Tillman. C.J. knew his furry friend was there for him. So, when Tillman took a turn for the worse, C.J. was there for him.

I woke up one Sunday morning to discover Tillman wasn't hogging his usual spot on the bed. Shoving my feet into a pair of slippers, I hurried downstairs, breathing a sigh of relief when I found him sleeping on the couch.

"You scared me," I said, stroking his soft head.

Tillman opened one eye and gave a half-hearted wag of his tail.

"Come on, buddy, let's get some breakfast."

That's when I noticed Tillman was struggling to get up.

"Need a little help?" I said, easing him off his side and onto his belly.

Tillman grunted, then stumbled off the couch and onto the floor. He was wobbly on his feet and his head dipped down on the left side as if he'd suffered a stroke. Immediately, I called the veterinarian but he was out of town. I spent most of that Sunday caring for my beloved dog as well as I could, then showed up at the vet's office first thing Monday morning. I wasn't going to wait for them to give me an appointment. This was an emergency.

"He had a stroke," the vet confirmed. "The best treatment for him is rest, decrease his stress, and bring him in for monthly injections for the next twelve months. Hopefully, he'll have a full recovery."

Thus, began Tillman's new season of life. His sight wasn't as clear as it was before the stroke and loud or unexpected noises seemed to cause him undue stress. So instead of bringing Tillman to see C.J. and his sisters, they came to visit him. He seemed to enjoy their company as long as they didn't get too rowdy. At times, I'd find C.J. sitting on the floor in the living-room, Tillman's head resting in his lap as he read him stories. Sometimes, the two of them would lay side by side on the couch, C.J.'s arm wrapped around his furry friend.

When C.J.'s mother was arrested, he and his sisters came to live with me for a while. Needless to say, Tillman was thrilled to have them around twenty-four/seven. He even switched from sleeping in my bed to sleeping in C.J.'s bed.

"You traitor," I would tease, as Tillman padded down the hall to C.J.'s room.

Tillman has mostly recovered from his stroke. His face still dips slightly to one side and he startles easily. When weather permits, he enjoys a ride in the car or short visits to the park.

Tillman has offered comfort, companionship, consolation, support, and friendship to so many people over the years. He's been a shoulder to cry on, a battle buddy to an anxious mother, and a listening ear in times of trouble. He was and is the original face and ambassador for *Dog's Nation.*

Chapter Eleven
Kearstyn

"A dog will teach you unconditional love.
If you can have that in your life, things won't be too bad."
Robert Wagner

Kearstyn was only ten when her father passed away. I met them when she and her siblings and mother lived in a women's shelter. They would come to the park every Wednesday and help me train the dogs that were currently housed at *Dog's Nation*. Please allow me to share her story, in her own words:

"Working at Shawn's after my dad passed away was helpful because my family was going through a rough time. With my mom's addiction and my dad not being there, we struggled a lot. Shawn was always there to take us kids in and let us help with the dogs. I learned at a young age that dogs can help a lot with depression and anxiety and PTSD. I don't think my dad's death affected me as much as the rest of my family, it was more my mom's drug addiction that impacted me. Mostly I tried to distract myself by going to Shawn's. She always had something for me to do and if we didn't have anything to do after cleaning the kennels and feeding the dogs and cleaning, filling up their water bowls, I would build a fort in the living room with Tillman and Maverick.

"I remember I would have nightmares quite often but the dogs helped with that a lot. Maverick and Tillman would snuggle with me on the couch and if I had a nightmare, I would whisper their names and they would curl up right next to me and let me hug them until I fell asleep.

"Working at *Dog's Nation* made me realize that dogs are an important part of my life. No matter what you're going through, no matter how sad you are, no matter what path you're taking in life, however many heartbreaks and breakdowns, through all the tears and through all the smiles, your dog will always be there wagging its tail when you open your front door, happy you're home safe. That's how I knew I had to have a dog when we moved to Nevada and I stopped going to Shawn's.

"I was recently diagnosed with severe depression and anxiety, bipolar disorder, and PTSD. Having dogs helped with all that quite a bit. I'm so happy I had the opportunity to work at *Dog's Nation* with Shawn. It taught me a lot of lessons in life, made me realize a lot of things, and changed my life. The best medicine is man's best friend.

"I am now proud to say that my mom has been clean and sober for seventeen months and I am getting the help that I need too. Thank you, *Dog's Nation* and Shawn Abell, for letting us take a part in your life, because you have changed ours and made it better for so many years."

Chapter Twelve
Trey

"I believe all animals were created by God to help keep man alive."
Iwao Fujita

Once a marine, always a marine. Tyler lived by this truism, yet sometimes he wished he could forget the horrors of the war in Iraq, even for just one day. Unfortunately, his body and mind couldn't cast aside the dreadful memories. There were nights when he woke up soaked in sweat, thrashing against the blankets, feeling as though they were pinning him down, a flashback of that fateful day when he was trapped under a five-thousand-pound armored Humvee.

As a military dog-handler in Iraq, Tyler and Luke, his Belgian Malinois, spent the bulk of their days searching for Improvised Explosive Devices. Theirs was a life of constant danger as they ferreted out and destroyed the deadly explosives. Luke's powerful sense of smell could sniff out the urea nitrate and hydrogen peroxide used in making IEDs from several feet away.

One day, after neutralizing over twenty IEDs, Tyler, Luke, and their two comrades headed back to base. One minute, they were discussing which foods they missed the most from back home, the next their Humvee was blown into the air like a toy in the hands of a toddler.

The heavy military vehicle landed on its side, pinning Tyler inside. The explosion was so loud, he couldn't hear anything except the ringing in his ears. Bits of shrapnel bit into his back, legs, and arms. Droplets of blood trickled down his cheek and into his mouth. Tyler tried to move, but his legs wouldn't respond. He struggled to focus, but when he lifted his head, the world went dark.

When he regained consciousness, he was laying on a cot at the base's mobile medical unit. A medic was standing beside his cot, injecting medications into his IV.

"You're a very lucky man," the medic told Tyler. "That dog saved your life."

"Where is Luke?" Tyler asked, struggling to sit up. All at once, the room began to spin. Tyler quickly laid back against the pillows.

A wet nose pressed itself against Tyler's hand. The soldier breathed a deep sigh of relief, stroking the dog's soft ears over and over.

"That dog pulled you out of the wreckage just in time. When the response team found your Humvee, there was nothing left but a burned-out shell. At first, they thought you were also dead, but then your dog let out a bark ..."

"Also dead?" Tyler interrupted.

"Yes. I'm sorry, I thought you knew. The other two members of your platoon died in the explosion."

Tyler let out a strangled cry. Brad's last comment about his mother's delicious blueberry pie instantly came to mind. Never again would he sit at his mother's table and enjoy a slice of her pie.

After treating him at the field hospital, Tyler was evacuated out of Iraq. Luke was cleared to accompany Tyler on the plane, lying beside his handler as they headed home. Back in the States, Tyler underwent several surgeries, his faithful dog Luke always beside him as he endured painful sessions of physical therapy and learned how to walk again. But Tyler would never be the same man again. He was eventually released from the military due to a permanent limp, traumatic brain injury, PTSD, seizures, and mobility issues.

Although Tyler was thankful Luke dragged him to safety, he lived with survivor's guilt. Why had he survived, but not Brad and Tony? At times, those feelings overwhelmed him to the point where he would explode with anger, punching his fist into a wall or kicking the trash can across the room.

Sometimes, he would wake up in the hospital having suffered another seizure. These episodes left him so weak, it was a struggle just to move from his bed to the kitchen for a glass of water. Tyler's wife did the best she could, under the circumstances. But she worked as a nurse at the local hospital which meant she was gone for ten to twelve hours at a time. Thankfully, Luke was there to help Tyler through every struggle-filled day.

As Luke aged, Tyler realized he needed another dog. Luke had not been trained to perform the tasks required of service dog. When a friend told him about *Dog's Nation* and our mission to provide service dogs to veterans with disabilities, Tyler immediately called.

Speaking with me over the phone, I could hear the anticipation in his voice.

"I'll do my best to find just the right dog for you," I said. "It may take some time because you'll need a larger dog for bracing purposes and taller dogs are not as readily available for adoption as small to medium-sized dogs."

Several days after my conversation with Tyler, I received a call from a shelter several counties away. They had a Great Dane-Lab mix ready for adoption. I didn't waste any time, but immediately drove out to fetch the dog. His name was Trey and he was a large, sturdy, muscular dog; a perfect match for Tyler. Now I had to determine whether or not Trey would be able to learn the special behaviors needed to assist with Tyler's specific needs and requirements.

After mastering the basics such as sit, lay down, stay, and so on, we moved on to other skills. I trained him how to go up the stairs, always one step above me, and taught him to remain on the same step as me on the way down. I exposed him to many sounds he and Tyler would encounter on their outings such as trucks, car horns, children laughing and yelling. I taught him the proper way to walk alongside a grocery cart, how to enter and exit a building, how to tap the handicapped door access button, and many other tasks so crucial to proper daily functions.

Part of Trey's training involved learning how to brace. Like a cane, the service dog is trained to offer support when walking or standing. When bracing, the dog must stand with his weight evenly distributed on all four feet, then tighten his muscles so the handler can lean on its shoulders when rising from a chair, getting out of a car, and so forth.

Trey also learned the "all-clear" and "cover" commands, performing a parameter check so no one moved in too close to Tyler's personal space or came up behind him or tapped him on the shoulder, actions which could send him into a full-blown panic attack.

Pretty soon, Tyler was actively participating in the training sessions, spending hours with Trey and me, learning and teaching the commands that would offer him the ability to resume a semi-independent life and get out instead of having to stay at home. After completing all the skills required as a service dog as well as the tasks specific to Tyler's needs, Trey was able to go to his forever home.

Shortly after Trey went to live with Tyler, the veteran experienced a seizure at the grocery store. Trey never hesitated. He knew exactly what to do, standing over his handler until help arrived.

Tyler and Trey were such a great team that the local veterans' association invited them to speak at a gathering, raising awareness and educating veterans on the benefits of owning a service dog. They were also invited to a local airport to educate their employees about assisting and improving services for service dog teams.

Tyler considers himself doubly blessed; one dog saved his life, the other gave him back his life. He is blessed indeed!

Chapter Thirteen
Chevron

"The average dog is nicer than the average person."
Andy Rooney

It never ceases to amaze me that dogs can endure terrible living conditions and even abuse at the hands of their owners, yet still retain that core ability to trust and love. I believe dogs, for the most part, are able to leave the past in the past and move on, savoring the pleasures of each new day to the fullest. I wish we humans could do the same.

When I received a call about a pit bull that needed rehoming, I was glad to adopt him. The poor dog, along with many others, had been living in atrocious conditions. Instead of using monetary donations to feed the dogs in her care, the woman who operated the supposed 'animal rescue' was keeping it for herself. When first responders arrived, they were horrified to find several dead dogs in various stages of decay and over a dozen dogs near starvation.

Chevron, a beautiful black pit bull with cropped ears, had discovered how to operate the slip latch on the dog crates, freeing himself and several others before rescuers arrived on the scene. He was found running loose and taken to a local shelter where he was treated and nursed back to health.

When Chevron came to *Dog's Nation*, he was still underweight and fairly shy. The first few days, we let him chill and adapt to his new surroundings. I would often find one of our volunteers sitting in his kennel run, talking and visiting with the newcomer. He never displayed any aggressive tendencies but seem to enjoy the company, laying with his chin on his front paws, ears perked, eyes surveying our comings and goings. Pretty soon, he was able to leave his kennel and was introduced to the other dogs. Like a shadow, he would trot along beside or behind me, following along wherever I went.

Like Tillman, I began to train Chevron, teaching him the skills and behaviors needed to become a service dog. He was a quick learner, a trait typical of the pit bull breed. His mellow temperament and gentle spirit made him a great candidate for a service dog. He and Tillman became friends, riding along in the car when I went to the park or to public venues, my ambassadors for *Dog's Nation*.

After Tillman's stroke, Chevron took up the torch. He and Monty helped me raise awareness and educate groups about service dogs. He enjoys people and never displays the slightest sign of rancor or ill will towards humans in general, despite those atrocious first months of his life.

It's not how he was raised, but how he survived that makes Chevron so incredibly special. His resilience and sweet character are a constant reminder that it's not what happened to you that defines you but who you choose to become. He might be a big, black, sixty-pound toughie on the outside, but on the inside he's just a cuddly teddy bear.

Chapter Fourteen
Metallica

"There is no exercise better for the heart
than reaching down and lifting people up."
John Holmes

My dad died ten days after he got out of prison. It affected me and my family pretty hard. We had a lot of family and friends supporting us throughout our grieving period. One of our friends that was there for us a lot was Shawn; we'd go over and stay with her at *Dog's Nation*.

When we were there, we helped her take care of the dogs, which helped distract us from our pain. The distraction is great when you have depression and the dogs were a big help because when you're down and you feel like you just want to end it all, it makes it a lot easier to keep going when you have a companion beside you and to know while you're training the dogs that it will go to someone who really needs him/her there as an amazing service dog.

Chapter Fifteen
Bambi

"God knew my heart needed you."
Tamara Berry

She was grieving. I could see it in the way she skulked past her food dish, uninterested in its contents, then flopped down near the front door. She just laid there on the cold tile floor, her mournful eyes watching as I picked up one of her chew toys.

"Want your ducky?" I said, squeezing the stuffed toy which emitted a strangled-sounding squawk.

Bambi let out a sigh and laid her head on her front paws. Her owners, Mr. and Mrs. Peterson, had died in a car accident, leaving behind their beloved chihuahua. With no official animal control in the small town of El Dorado Springs, I was the one they called to rescue orphaned pets.

Seeing as the dog appeared to be quite young, I had every confidence I could train her and possibly find her a new home. I quickly gathered her bed, her toys, and her food dishes and stowed them in the back of my car, then went back into the house to fetch Bambi. She didn't object when I scooped her up in my arms and carried her out to my car. It would take time and a lot of love, but the little sand-colored chihuahua would gradually heal and possibly care for someone else as much as she'd loved the Petersons.

Sure enough, Bambi quickly learned all the skills and behaviors necessary for her to become a service dog. Though tiny in stature, she had a huge heart, a grand personality, and a clever mind. Skills that typically took several weeks for some dogs to learn, she mastered in half that time.

When I met Julia, a young woman battling brain cancer, I sensed Bambi would be a good match for her. Julia's physician felt she would benefit from owning a service dog that could assist her physically as well as emotionally. Julia had no use for a medium to large sized dog but wanted a smaller dog she could hold in her arms and cuddle during chemo treatments.

Bambi and Julia quickly forged a strong friendship as they worked with me, learning all the commands and behaviors I'd taught Bambi so they could become an effective team. Finally, one beautiful autumn day, Bambi moved to her new home.

Because of her condition, Julia's emotions frequently changed throughout the course of each day. Bambi would sense her owner's plunging moods before Julia even realized it herself. The little chihuahua would run circles around Julia and bark frantically until her owner took the medications that alleviated the worst of her angst and despair.

Julia was so enamored with her new helper; she wrote the following article which was published in the local paper:

What a service dog is to me
Not every dog can be a service dog.
Dogs come in many shapes, sizes and breeds.
They only need a big heart and a willingness to serve and love.
My service dog, Bambi, recently helped me during a crisis.
All I had to do was put on her vest and she did her job.
She laid on me, licked my face, and got me to pet her, and soon I was laughing and we were playing.
All of the negative thoughts were gone and I was able to think clearly.
We had gone through our first crisis and came out with flying colors.
Hurray for Bambi, what a team!

When they went for walks on chilly days, Julia tucked Bambi in her sweater to keep her warm. During Julia's chemo treatments, Bambi curled up on her lap, a comfort and solace in the midst of her darkest hours. And during those long hours of the night, when sleep eluded her and cancer took its toll on her body and mind, Bambi stayed right beside her. Bambi was truly the best medicine for Julia's troubled soul.

Sadly, the tumor in Julia's brain continued to grow. Eventually, Julia was incapable of caring for herself and had to be hospitalized. She was in tears as I came to collect Bambi.

"I'll make sure she comes to visit you regularly," I promised.

Sure enough, Bambi was always excited when I mentioned a trip to the hospital. Instead of wagging her tail, she would wiggle her entire rear end with anticipation. She quickly became well-known, as well as a favorite among the hospital staff. She would greet everyone we met on the way to Julia's room, then settle into the crook of Julia's arm once I set her on the bed. Though sedated most of the time, Julia occasionally responded to her dog's presence by whispering a slurred, "Love Bambi."

Several months after Julia's passing, a friend told me about Mia, an older woman who had lost her husband and desperately wanted a smaller dog to keep her company and help her with basic tasks. When Mia came to *Dog's Nation* for a visit, she was immediately attracted to Bambi. Maybe the older woman reminded Bambi of Mrs. Peterson, but it was love at first sight for both of them. I was a little concerned, seeing as they were both getting along in years, but there was no denying the two were smitten with each other.

Several weeks later, I received a letter from Mia, along with several photos. If I'd entertained any concerns about the dog's new home they were quickly set to rest. It seemed the little chihuahua was leading a very active social life, travelling here and there with her new owner. From beaches to mountains, to cruise ships, Bambi and Mia seemed to be having a good time together. One of the pictures showed Bambi sitting beside the newly-crowned Miss Missouri, posing as though he were the star of the show.

Bambi is a good reminder that stature is not half as important as the size of one's heart. He had more love to give than any other dog or human I've ever met. As Julia would have said, "Hooray for Bambi!"

Chapter Sixteen
Eleven Cats and a Lawyer

"There is nothing in the world so irresistibly contagious as laughter and good humor."
Charles Dickens

"Shawn? This is Adam Weller. Can you meet me at the courthouse in an hour?"

Adam was an attorney I'd met at an autism awareness fair. He was impressive, standing over six feet tall and built like a quarterback. His deep voice made me think of James Earl Jones. Today, he sounded rushed.

"Hello, Adam. What's going on?"

"I need you to come fetch some cats. Their owners, who are also my clients, were arrested this morning and I can't leave the cats alone."

I sensed there was something he wasn't telling me. "You do realize cats aren't like dogs? You can leave them for a day or two and they'll be fine. Don't your clients have family who can take the cats?"

"Not that I know of. Listen, I really need you to come as soon as possible. I have to be in court in a couple of hours."

"Listen, Adam. Why don't you cut to the chase? What is really going on here? Why the urgency?"

Adam let out a loud sigh. "Okay, Shawn. Truth is, my clients were evicted from their home a week ago. They've been living in their car along with their cats —."

He paused and let out another sigh. "— all eleven of them."

"I... I'm sorry. Did you just say eleven cats? In a car? For a week?"

"That's what I said. The worst of it is that my clients were arrested in El Dorado and I had to drive out there to retrieve their car and their cats."

"What were they driving? A cat-illac?" Sometimes, I crack myself up.

"That's a good one, Shawn. Unfortunately, there's nothing funny about this situation. My suit is covered with fur and I can't get rid of the reek of ammonia and cat feces from my nostrils."

I was trying hard not to laugh, but it was really hard. "I'm sorry, Adam. I shouldn't be laughing about your cat-astrophy."

I heard another sigh, louder this time.

"How am I supposed to find eleven cat crates and drive thirty-six miles to Bolivar within the next hour? Anyone there who might have some pet crates you could borrow?"

"We have some cardboard file boxes you could use. Tape the lids shut so the cats don't escape during the transfer and pop the handles open so they have some air. Oh, and bring a lint brush if you have one."

"Right. Give me a few minutes to finish up here, then I'll meet you at the courthouse."

"Thanks a million, Shawn. I owe you one."

"Hey, that's what I'm here for. Just do me a favor, Adam."

"What's that?"

"If you see a stray dog, run."

The line went dead. I hung up, still laughing at the thought of Adam, looking a bit green around the gills, driving thirty-six miles in a car full of cats. He never did like felines in the first place. Now he would probably loath them.

After collecting several cat crates from my garage and enlisting the help of one of the volunteers, I headed to Bolivar. When I pulled up in front of the courthouse, I noticed a tow truck parked behind a grey Chevy HHR. Adam was talking with the tow-truck driver, his hands flying left and right, up and down, as he spoke. Adam would make a good Frenchman.

"This the car?" I asked, carrying a cat crate in each hand. I set them beside the Chevy then peered through the back window. Two grey-and-white kittens were draped over the back seat. In the cargo area, a black cat nursed a litter of kittens.

"You bring the lint brush?" Adam said by way of greeting.

"No, Adam. That was the least of my worries. Don't you have a secretary or a paralegal who could run to the dollar store and get one for you?"

"My secretary is out of the office today, and my paralegal is tied up."

"Find some duct tape, then. Nice and sticky. Works great."

"Thanks, I'll try that."

"You guys mind getting a move on?" the truck driver said, glaring at both of us. "I have a schedule to keep."

"Right. Sorry," I said, raising the hatch. The smell of cat urine and feces hit like a backed-up drain field.

Behind me, the tow-truck driver staggered backwards, then turned and vomited in the bushes. I was feeling a little nauseous myself.

"How did you manage?" I asked, turning towards Adam.

"Mind over matter," he said, snagging an orange tabby that was slinking towards freedom. "Oh no, you don't." With one swift movement, he grabbed the cat by the nape, pushed him into one of the crates I'd brought with me, then slammed the carrier door closed and latched it.

"Wow! That was pretty impressive!" I said, gathering two young cats into the second carrier. They were small enough to be roomies until we got back to *Dog's Nation*.

Karen, the volunteer I'd brought along to help me, trotted over with two more carriers. I grabbed one and quickly filled it with mama cat and all three kittens. In no time, we had all eleven cats secured.

"You okay over there?" I called out to the tow-truck driver who was looking a little pale.

"If one of you could slip the car into neutral, I'd be very grateful."

Adam had the kindness to put the car in neutral. "All done and ready to go."

The driver gave him a thumbs up, then hoisted the car and towed it off.

"You know I can't keep all these cats," I told Adam.

"I'll contact a group I know to spay and neuter them, then get them off your hands as soon as I can. Hopefully, we can adopt them all out fairly quickly."

"Your clients won't want them back?"

"I wouldn't count on it. Even though I am the best lawyer in town, they're both looking at ten to fifteen years of jail time."

"Well, I guess that answers that," I said, turning to head back to my car.

"Cat-egorically."

I spun around. Adam was grinning like the Cheshire cat in *Alice in Wonderland*.

"Well played," I offered, returning the smile.

As I opened my car door, the roll of masking tape I usually keep in the side pocket of the door caught my eye. Snatching it up, I called out, "Adam!"

He turned back.

"Catch!" I said, tossing him the roll.

He snagged the tape as it sailed through the air.

"Not a lint brush but second best," I said.

I climbed into my car amid a chorus of cat wails. Turning the key in the ignition, I glanced at Karen and let out a loud sigh. "This is going to be a long drive home."

"That's fur sure."

Our eyes met over the top of two file boxes stacked between us on the front seat and both erupted into a fit of laughter. Humor definitely helps in my line of work. Maybe Adam's too, for that matter.

Chapter Seventeen
Journey

"The journey of life is sweeter
when traveled with a dog."
Bridget Willoughby

The shrill ring of the phone woke me from a deep sleep. Glancing at the bright red numbers glowing in the darkness, I groaned; three o'clock in the morning. *This can't be good,* I thought, snatching up the receiver.

"Hello," I mumbled, voice groggy from sleep. Although I was on call twenty-four/seven, my mind wasn't always at its clearest in the wee hours of the morning.

"Sorry. Did I wake you?" a timid voice asked.

"It's okay," I said, politely. Anyone who had cause to call me at this hour must be in dire need. "How can I help you?"

The woman on the other end of the line broke into sobs. I heard her talking to someone, then a baritone voice travelled down the line. "Hi, this is

Patrick. My wife, Rebecca, is a little emotional right now. We've spent the last three hours looking for our son." There was a catch in his voice. "Thankfully, he's okay. A police officer found him wandering through the woods near our house."

I hated to think about all the kids who have wandered off and never made it home. "Has your son done this before?"

"Jared has autism. He's wandered off several times, despite the locks on the doors and windows. My wife and I sleep with one eye open most of the time, but tonight he managed to slip past me." His voice wavers. "I usually sleep on the couch so I can hear him if he tries to skip out, but he hadn't run off in a while, so I figured I'd go back to sleeping in my own bed. I should have known better."

"It's not your fault," I said, fully awake now. I'd heard this same story over and over. Parents desperately trying to keep their children alive and blaming themselves for their child's unpredictable behaviors. "You're doing the best you can."

"My wife quit her job when Jared was diagnosed with autism spectrum disorder. She teaches him at home and an ABA therapist visits every week, but nothing seems to work. He doesn't speak, can't stand to be touched, and almost anything can trigger a massive meltdown, even the noise the heater makes when it starts to cycle."

Hypersensitivity can be one of the most difficult facets of autism to deal with. Other than providing a child with a quiet environment and very little change in routine, there's not a whole lot parents can do to alleviate their child's discomfort. Some wear sunglasses indoor and out, as well as noise-cancelling headphones to cope with household noises such as the hum of the refrigerator or the ticking of the clock. But with extreme hypersensitivity, life often becomes unbearable for many individuals on the spectrum.

"Is Jared home now?" I asked.

"Yes. They took him to the hospital after they found him walking through the woods wearing only a tee shirt and shorts. No shoes, no socks. But he's home now."

I shivered at the thought. It was January and although it hadn't snowed in a couple of weeks, the ground was still frozen. He could so easily have died of hypothermia.

"A friend of ours gave us your number," he continued. "Told us you train autism service dogs."

"Yes, that's what we do."

"Thing is, we can't afford $25,000.00 for a dog."

"We don't charge anything at *Dog's Nation*. It's part of our mission."

I heard a woof of air as he expelled a deep breath. This often takes people by surprise. "How old is Jared?"

"He's ten."

"How is he with animals?"

"Oh, he loves them. We have two cats."

I made a mental note to make sure we paired Jared with a dog who didn't mind cats, then asked a bit about Jared's diagnosis, his greatest issues, and his living environment, as well as the usual questions I run through when vetting a prospective owner. I needed to ensure every one of the dogs I trained went to good homes.

I also told Jared's father I would need a note from his son's physician with his official diagnosis along with a letter recommending the boy get a service dog to prevent self-harming behaviors, de-escalate meltdowns, and ensure personal safety.

After promising Jared's father I would be in contact, I set to work searching for just the right dog. Jared would need a service dog that was big enough and strong enough to block him if he tried to run off, that was good with cats, and didn't mind younger kids as Jared was the oldest of three.

After contacting various shelters in the area as well as in other states, I eventually received a call from an animal rescue in Illinois. They had a Labrador-

Golden Retriever mix who was supposed to be euthanized the next day. When the shelter coordinator, a friend of mine named Mary, heard my special request and saw the kennel card that indicated he was good with cats, she sensed this dog might be the right one for Jared.

Thus, began Journey's new life. After spending months training him to block, anchor, de-escalate a meltdown, negotiate parking lots, watch his boy at the playground and many other tasks specific to autism service dogs, Journey was finally ready to meet his new owner. Jared and Journey took to each other like a bear to honey. There was no doubt that Journey was born to become this boy's best friend and guardian.

Several weeks later, I received an update from Jared's mother. With Journey's help, their son was finally beginning to come out of his shell.

"Those two are inseparable," she said. I could hear joy and relief in her voice. "They sleep together, play together, and do everything together. We even took Jared and Journey to one of Alissa's basketball games at school. With the help of noise-cancelling headphones and Journey to keep him seated, we were able to stay till halftime. That's a big feat for Jared! Needless to say, Alissa was thrilled to have her whole family there to watch her play."

"I'm so glad Journey worked out for your son. He's a special dog that just needed a special boy to love," I said, struggling not to cry. This time I was the one choking up on the phone. But they were tears of happiness.

These are the miracles that make *Dog's Nation* so valuable and unique. In the process of saving one life, we often save two. And that makes every day worthwhile.

Chapter Eighteen
Gorda

"Out of difficulties grow miracles."
Jean de la Bruyère

A low thrum intruded on the early afternoon hush, the noise increasing to a loud rumble as the small plane broke through a patch of plump white clouds. It circled twice, then banked right, tipping its wings as the brisk wind buffeted the aircraft. With masterful precision, the plane descended, back wheels then front wheels touching down, the engines screaming in protest as the pilot engaged its reverse thrust, slowing its forward momentum. The cargo plane gradually slowed and came to a halt in front of the large, metal hanger where I sat waiting.

Several months ago, I'd received a call from a woman named Barbara, who worked at an animal shelter in Manhattan, New York. She was wondering if I would be willing to take in a Staffordshire Terrier.

"Her owner died of AIDS," Barbara added, knowing this was an issue for some people. In that day and age, the myths regarding AIDS had not yet been debunked.

The pit bull mix was born in the streets of New York, in the aftermath of 9-11. Found cowering behind a dumpster down an alley in Manhattan, she was taken to a nearby shelter where she was put up for adoption. A woman named Marion visited the shelter and fell in love with Gorda's cute face and placid brown eyes.

Now that Marion had passed away, Gorda needed a new home. Barbara had heard *Dog's Nation* welcomed Pit bulls, so she decided to give me a call to see if I would consider adopting Gorda. Around that time, our nation was slowly emerging from a stigma which deeply affected individuals who were HIV positive. Many dogs, whose owners died from AIDS, were automatically euthanized. My own family had suffered from misconceptions surrounding AIDS when one of my cousins contracted the disease. She was ostracized, secluded behind a glass cubicle at work, excluded from public functions and shunned by people who were previously her friends, all because of fallacies about the disease.

I knew better and agreed to take the dog. "I would love to adopt Gorda."

After my phone conversation with Barbara, several months passed without any news. I assumed the dog had been adopted out or euthanized. Then, out of the blue, I received a call asking if I could meet a cargo plane landing at Eldon Airfield the next day, around one in the afternoon, as Gorda would be on board.

Now here I was at the tiny airport, watching as the two-man crew unloaded a large crate and wheeled it over to my car.

"This your dog, ma'am?" a man in blue coveralls asked, squinting against the brisk wind, his cheeks red with cold.

"Is this Gorda?" I asked, tugging my coat collar closer about my face.

The man checked the luggage tag. "That's what the ticket says."

"Then, yes, this is my dog. Could you please load her into the car?" I wasn't about to let the dog loose in the hanger. I had no idea how she might react.

"The vet gave her something to calm her during the flight so she's still a bit groggy," the attendant said, transferring the crate into the cargo area in the back of my SUV.

"Thank you. Hopefully, she will sleep most of the way home," I said, closing the hatch.

A few snowflakes drifted downward as I drove home, soft, lazy flakes drifting down upon the earth like powdered sugar on a cake, then melting as soon as they hit the windshield. I hoped the heavier snow would hold off until I reached home. Winter had lingered in our little corner of the world and though the first daffodils had popped up, we were still dealing with snow flurries and bitterly cold winds. Though James, my helper at *Dog's Nation* loved the winter months, I was more than ready for spring.

Pulling into my driveway, I heard a rustle and a low whine emanating from the back. Gorda was awake and ready to get out of her crate.

"It's okay, sweetheart," I said, parking the car in front of my house. "You're finally home. No more traveling."

I slipped from the car, turned up my coat collar, then opened the hatch. A shiny black nose poked through the bars of the cage, twitching as she took in new smells.

"Welcome to the country," I said, lifting her crate out of the car. She wasn't light and it took all the muscle I had to heft her up the porch steps and into the house.

I didn't know much about Gorda, so I chose to leave her in the carrier for just a while longer while she acclimated to her new surroundings. Of course, the other dogs were eager to meet her, but I put them out back to allow Gorda to adjust to her new home in peace.

Gorda was a magnificent dog, a typical Staffordshire Terrier with a stocky, muscular body, short tail, cropped ears set high on her broad head. Her shiny black coat sported a dash of white on her broad chest. She was a little wobbly on her legs from sedation but otherwise seemed fairly keen on exploring the house.

After a quick potty-break out front, Gorda sniffed her way around the house to the back where the other dogs greeted her through the fence. They seemed quite pleased with our new addition, their tails whipping back and forth in greeting. She had officially been welcomed and accepted into their midst.

Gorda was very intelligent and a fast learner, quickly integrating into our family and work routine. For the first month, we walked her around the park, training her on a lead while exposing her to various noises such as loud trucks driving past, the squeal of brakes as vehicles stopped at the traffic light, and focusing on her tasks without getting distracted.

After she'd mastered her public access training, I took her to local shops, training her how to walk beside a cart and introducing her to various floor textures, such as carpet and linoleum. Some dogs are scared when they see the fluorescent lights reflected on the linoleum, but Gorda took it all in stride.

She enjoyed her trips to the community center where she learned how to ride the elevator, walk up and down the grate-type stairs, walk around the rubberized track, and gradually got used to the banging of weights in the weight room, the loud fan in the exercise room and the air-conditioner kicking in on hot, summer days.

After months of intensive training, Gorda graduated and became an official ambassador for *Dog's Nation*. She attended functions with me, providing opportunities to educate and raise awareness about service dogs, PTSD, and Autism Spectrum Disorder. Her adoption precipitated a working relationship with several rescue organizations around the country and caused many to rethink their preconceptions about pit bulls.

Several months after Gorda came into my life, I received another call from the rescue group in Manhattan who had flown her out to Eldon Airfield. They had another pit bull they needed to rehome. At one point in the conversation, I asked the woman I was speaking with to relay a message to Barbara. I wanted her to know all the good Gorda had brought to my life and other people's lives as well.

"Barbara? We don't have a Barbara here," the woman informed me.

"It would have been about a year ago. Maybe she's moved?" I suggested.

"I'm sorry, Ms. Abell, but I've been working here for twelve years and we've never had anyone named Barbara work for us."

To say I was shaken up would be putting it lightly. Who was this woman who had saved Gorda and sent her to me, thus opening numerous and unexpected doors for me to educate and raise awareness about the hope service dogs can bring to individuals with special-needs?

All I know is that I am thankful for Barbara and her wonderful gift. Gorda has brought hope, joy, and comfort to so many individuals whose lives she's touched. She's my furry, four-legged, heaven-sent miracle.

Chapter Nineteen
Monty

"When an eighty-five-pound mammal licks your tears away,
Then tries to sit on your lap,
It's hard to feel sad".
Kristan Higgins

The first time I set eyes on Monty, I knew he was a survivor. Despite the massive wounds covering his body and the line of angry red blotches running along the top of his head, the Pitbull mix lay quietly on the front seat of the rusty, old red pickup truck, his tongue lolling from the heat.

"Neighbors dumped him on us," the man said, rolling a toothpick back and forth across his lips. Dark smudges stained his hands and his tank top was streaked with black smears. He smelled of engine oil. "Reckon they thought we'd care for it, but the wife and I don't want 'im."

"What's his name?" I asked, trying to rein in a growing sense of irritation. This poor dog had obviously been mistreated for quite some time, judging from the scabs and ugly red sores along his face and back.

"Monty." The man pulled the toothpick from his mouth and pointed it at the dog. "So, you want him or not?"

I knew what future awaited Monty if I didn't. "Yea, I'll take him. What caused all these sores and the huge knot in the middle of his forehead?"

"Don't know. Don't care," he said, shoving the toothpick back into his mouth. "Just wanna get rid of the mutt."

I stepped forward to get a closer look at the dog. Head resting on his paws, he just laid there, staring at nothing in particular, as though he'd disassociated himself from the world in general.

"Hey Monty," I said in a gentle, soothing tone. "Welcome to your new home."

The dog picked up his head and turned to look at me. He probably wasn't used to kind voices.

"What's that big lump on the side of his neck?" I said, noticing the growth.

He shrugged. "Like I told 'ya. I don't know nothin' 'bout this dog. Honest."

"What about his previous owners?"

"You ain't gonna get nothin' from them. They up and left two days ago. Moved east somewhere."

With a sigh of frustration, I patted my leg. "Come on, Monty."

The dog sat up and looked at me expectantly.

"Come on," I said. "It's okay."

In spite of the obvious abuse, Monty was an impressive dog. Muscular and built like a tank, he could appear intimidating to many people who weren't familiar with Staffordshire Bull Terriers. But as he jumped from the truck, all I could see was a loveable animal who had fallen into the wrong hands.

"Come on, let's go find you something to drink," I said, moving towards the stoop where I always keep a bowl of clean water. Monty gave a guarded wag of his tail, then loped after me, tongue hanging out the side of his mouth. Once he spotted the bowl of water, he took several noisy slurps, spilling a good portion of it onto the porch.

I watched as the man climbed into his truck and drove off without saying goodbye, then eased myself to a crouch, close enough to communicate to Monty that I wouldn't hurt him, yet not too close to cause him alarm. The dog's massive head swiveled towards me, eyes alert and ears erect.

"It's okay, Monty. You're in a good place now," I said, holding out my hand, palm up, for him to sniff.

There was something magnetic about this dog, an instant connection I couldn't deny. For some reason, he reminded me of myself; maybe it was the survivor spirit or that drive to forget the bad and get on with life.

Warily, Monty slinked towards me then sniffed my hand.

"What happened to you out there?" I said, eyeing his sores. "Were you in a dog fight? Did your owner abuse you?"

Monty looked up at me, his big brown eyes so gentle and trusting. It was as though he sensed he'd found someone who would love him.

The following day, I whisked Monty off to the vet. Unfortunately, I had to leave him there; the vet had to perform surgery on his neck without delay. I felt bad for abandoning him so soon after his arrival, especially because he'd trusted me.

I found it hard to concentrate the rest of that day, throwing myself into my chores with renewed fervor, intent on distracting myself so I wouldn't ruminate on Monty's fate. Obviously, this dog had been through some terrible ordeal and though he appeared big and tough, he seemed to possess a peaceful, gentle spirit. I had no doubt Monty would prove to be smart, intelligent, and loyal – if he survived the surgery and it didn't turn out to be cancer.

The noonday heat eventually drove me indoors. I had just finished lunch when the vet called me. "Someone stabbed your poor dog in the neck," he said, without preamble. "I drained and cleaned the laceration, then sutured it closed. Also pulled a bullet from the back of his head. I've cleaned the wound and placed a couple of stitches there as well but he'll have to be on antibiotics for a while."

"A bullet?" I couldn't believe what I'd just heard. "Someone shot and stabbed him?"

"Actually, Monty was shot more than once," the vet said. "That line of sores along the top of his head are from bullets that ricocheted. This dog is very lucky to be alive."

"I'd say so!" My voice was growing in pitch. I took a deep breath to calm my nerves then resumed our discussion in a lower voice. "What about his open wounds?"

"They're bite marks. Some of them appear to be from a stallion, others look more like dog bites. He's also missing three eye teeth and several others are broken."

I felt like punching a wall. Instead, I paced up and down the kitchen.

"Can I come get him today or does he need to stay overnight?

"No. You can fetch him around closing time. The anesthesia should have worn off by then."

Monty was overjoyed when I went to pick him up. Tail swiping back and forth like a metronome set on Allegro, he trotted along beside me to the car. After I'd lifted him in, he climbed onto the front passenger seat as though that was his rightful place.

"So, you're one of those dogs, eh?" I said, laughing. "You like to co-pilot rather than stay in the back where you belong, don't you?" I didn't have the heart to banish him to the back seat. This poor boy had gone through enough for now.

On the way home, I kept sneaking occasional peeks at this miracle dog riding shotgun. Once he healed up, he would be a beautiful pit bull mix with a blue patch over one eye and blue markings along his strong, muscular body.

"Like the vet said, you are one lucky dog," I said, patting him gently on the head.

Monty laid down on the seat and let out a deep sigh, resting his head on his paws. He seemed quite alert for just having had a bullet removed from his head and several open wounds stitched up. If he was as sharp as I thought he was, he would be fairly easy to train. Although I could not release him as a service dog to an individual because of possible health complications from the injuries, Monty would be a wonderful dog to take with me to events to raise awareness.

"Want to make a quick stop off at the post-office?" I asked him. I had a parcel I wanted to ship off as soon as possible and Monty appeared to be doing quite well despite his surgery.

Monty wagged his tail in response, then let out a loud yawn.

"Okay, Monty. Show me what you've got."

Slipping the training vest over his head, I clipped a lead to it, then lifted him out of the car so he wouldn't rip open his stitches. Tail whipping back and forth, he padded alongside me, responding to my every cue as if he'd been doing this for years.

"You're making this look way too easy," I said, glancing at this sweet dog who was already tugging at my heart strings.

Of course, he knew it. He trotted into the post office with me as though this were a walk in the park, stood quietly beside me at the counter, and even drew praise from the staff and other customers.

"Don't you let all that praise go to your head," I told him, as we strode back to the car. Gently, I lifted him and placed him in the passenger seat. Closing his eyes, he let out a large yawn and drifted off to sleep.

Within days, Monty had slipped into a daily routine. He went everywhere with me. He quickly learned how to walk beside the food cart when I took him to the store. At the local fast-food restaurant I instructed him to sit while I ordered a meal, then lay by my feet while I ate. I took him to the park so he could grow accustomed to the loud trucks driving past as well as the hiss of their breaks as they stopped for the red light. In the community building, Monty learned how to mount the grid-like stairs, ride the elevator, walk the track, and get used to the various noises. Every new lesson he took in stride, quick to learn and eager to please.

Monty is still discovering all the ins and outs of life as a service dog, but his innate trust and his eagerness to master new skills have made him a pleasure to train. He is a constant reminder not to let labels define your character or adversities dictate your character. We are who we are by birth. We become who we are by choice.

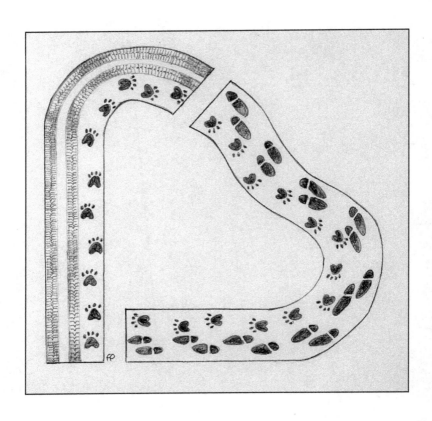

Chapter Twenty
Winter

"The best way to not feel hopeless is to get up and do something.
Don't wait for good things to happen to you.
If you go out and make some good things happen,
you will fill the world with hope,
you will fill yourself with hope."
Barack Obama

I met James through Pathways, a health organization which offers counseling and support to individuals who have undergone physical and emotional trauma. James' counselor had suggested volunteering with a charity or non-profit could potentially help him manage his time in a productive way, impart new skills, boost his self-confidence, and impact other people's lives as well as his own. When James discovered *Second Chance Barnyard* - the original name for *Dog's Nation* - was looking for volunteers, he jumped at the opportunity. He had always loved animals, especially dogs, and working with them seemed like a dream come true.

It was gratifying to see James invest so much time and energy into these dogs. The shy, reserved, unkempt young man who'd showed up on that first day gradually blossomed into a confident, happy, and well-groomed worker. James' story is one of childhood abuse and abandonment. To see him turn his life around and come this far is a miracle in itself. I'm proud to call him friend.

Born in Germany, June 28th, 1977, James was raised on the military base where his father was stationed. When he was two, his father walked out, abandoning his wife and two young children in a foreign country, far from family and friends. Fortunately, his mother, Lisa, was able to find a job working at the consulate. But her meager salary was barely sufficient to provide for a family of three.

One day, a young American soldier named Butch walked into the consulate, looking for help with some paperwork. Glancing up from her computer, Lisa noticed the young American standing at the counter, waiting, and ushered him over to her desk. When the smart-looking soldier with the intense brown eyes and lopsided grin invited her to go out for a drink after work, she immediately accepted. Soon they were seeing each other on a regular basis.

Eventually, Butch packed his scant belongings and moved in with them.

Given that both Butch and Lisa longed to return to the United States, Butch started making arrangements for all of them to be transferred back to America. But there was a hitch that needed to be remedied before any paperwork could be approved; although James was born on June 28, 1977, in a German civilian hospital, the United States didn't register his birth until July 1978. A paternity test had to be performed to confirm the identity of his biological father. Once that was established, the family was cleared to return to the States.

Back in Kansas, life spiraled out of control, going from bad to worse as his mom and step-dad got in with the wrong crowd and started taking opiates. James was only six years old when Butch introduced him to drugs. That was Butch's way of bonding with the young boy, or so he believed. Shortly after his eighth birthday, James' mom and stepdad were arrested for drug possession.

Now wards of the state, James and his sister were placed in a foster home. The man of the house insisted they call him 'Uncle Jack' even though they weren't related. 'Uncle Jack' was a hard man, demanding and harsh with his discipline. James noticed his sister becoming more and more reserved and quiet, pulling away from her brother when he asked if she was okay. One day, James walked in the house to find 'Uncle Jack' molesting his sister. James' efforts to protect his sister were met with brutal force, and he was also molested.

After two months of ruthless abuse, the authorities discovered what was happening and pulled James and his sister from the foster home. The kids were sent to live with their biological father who had returned to the States. When James and his sister told their father what had happened to them in the foster home, he simply shrugged and said, "deal with it. Life is hard and pain will only make you stronger." He then proceeded to abuse them as well. James and his sister agreed to never speak of the issue again. Doing so, only seemed to make their situation worse.

When he was nine, James' mother was released from prison. He and his sister were given a choice to go back to live with their mother or stay with their biological father. James chose to go back to live with his mother, while his sister opted to stay with her dad. For James, life was as bad as it could get. By the time he was fifteen, James was fed up with all the physical and mental abuse his stepfather dealt him. He wanted out.

But James feared for his half-sister who was only four years old. Because his mom and stepfather were either drunk or high most of the time, James took care of his little sister, fixing meals, washing clothes, and protecting her from his stepfather's irrational rampages. James was afraid his little sister or his mom would be seriously hurt or even die as a result of Butch's rage. Every night, James would hide his head under his pillow to shut out the loud arguments, the fights, and the terrified screams. "Make it stop, make it stop," he prayed over and over.

One day, when Butch went after his mom with clenched fists, James stepped in between his stepfather and mother. "Leave her alone!" he yelled. "We've had enough of your abuse."

"This is none of your business!" Butch roared, his face red with rage. "Get out of the way or get out of my house."

James stood his ground, firm in his resolve to protect his mom. Furious at his defiance, Butch spun on his heel and stormed down the hallway to James' room. Within seconds, James' possessions were destroyed. Stomping down the hall, Butch continued his destructive rampage in the kitchen, smashing dishes and tearing the doors off the cabinets. James exploded. Grabbing Butch by the collar, he tossed him through the living-room window, then jumped out after him, tackling his stepfather to the ground, standing over him so Butch couldn't get back into the house.

Within minutes, their driveway was swarming with first responders and police officers. After interrogating Butch and James, one of the officers approached James' mom and offered her a choice; Butch or James. She chose Butch.

Sullen, hurt, wounded, and brokenhearted, James packed his military duffle bag and left with a little stray dog he'd adopted named Dusty. James and Dusty survived by sleeping behind churches in the area and scrounging for food. Determined to finish high-school, James attended classes during the day and worked odd jobs in the evenings. His persistence and dedication paid off when he walked across the high-school platform and received his diploma. There was no one there to cheer for him or stand beside the tall, lanky youth for a photo to commemorate the momentous occasion. Yet, despite it all, James was proud of his accomplishment.

James was eventually discovered by a pastor who found him sleeping behind his church. The pastor drove James to a shelter in Salina, Kansas. At least he would have a roof over his head and a warm meal to fill his belly.

Dusty, James' faithful companion and the one friend who kept him going for the three years they were homeless, was failing. The dog was seventeen years old and in very poor health, so James made the heart-rending decision to have him put to sleep. It was time and James didn't want his friend to suffer any longer.

In 1999, James moved to Missouri. He worked for a mechanic, cleaning and helping with some of the repairs, one of the few good things he'd learned from his stepfather. But living on the streets had its toll on James' health. He had to undergo multiple surgeries which prevented him from keeping a permanent job. His pain was so intense, he had no option but to take opioids. He quickly grew addicted but chose a better path than his mother and stepfather. Instead of giving in to his body's cravings, James sought help. Through Pathways, he learned alternative strategies to help cope with chronic pain.

As he got more and more involved with *Dog's Nation*, James learned two important lessons; he had a passion for rescue dogs and working with the animals helped distract his mind from the pain, a valuable alternative to drugs. Under Shawn's guidance and tutoring he learned how to care for the dogs and how to train them to become service dogs. And every moment he spent with these animals brought him joy, something he hadn't experienced much growing up.

In 2003, James' health took a dive. He started losing feeling in his left leg. By 2005, he was confined to a wheelchair. The doctors predicted he would never be able to walk again. I could see him slipping into a state of despair and feared he might revert to his old ways. When he didn't show up one day, I loaded three dogs into my car and drove to his house. When James opened the door, I informed him that I needed him to get back to work.

"I have several veterans who desperately needed service dogs and are still waiting on you and me to complete their dogs' training," I said.

"How can I help you when I can't even get out of this wheelchair?" he objected, pushing the door closed.

I wedged the door open with my foot. "Actually, you are the best person to help me with the dogs. Aren't we training them how to walk beside a wheelchair? Don't we teach them how to push the automatic door button for their handlers? And who's going to train them how to maneuver ramps, elevators, and wheelchair accessible walkways? You! That's who."

Sheepishly, James conceded I had a point. I packed him into the car along with his wheelchair and thus commenced a new phase of training for both

James and the service dogs that would be paired with individuals who were confined to a wheelchair.

In the process of training the service dogs, I noticed how much James loved them and how his mood improved when he was with them. He, himself, needed a service dog to help him live a more efficient and productive life. After receiving a note from his physician confirming his handicap and need for a service dog, I offered him the choice between three dogs. He chose a beautiful husky named Winter. She was energetic, loving, and a quick learner. In fact, she was awarded the Good Canine Citizen Award and was one of the smartest dogs I've ever trained. She'd been found, abandoned, in a trailer for who knows how many days. Yet she'd moved on, unwilling to let her past define her, just as James was learning to do.

I am forever grateful James chose to volunteer at *Dog's Nation* all those years ago. Working at *Dog's Nation* has given him a new lease on life. He's grown and flourished as a person. He's defied the doctors' prognosis and, with Winter's help, has regained some of his mobility. With her by his side, James was able to exchange his wheelchair for a cane, knowing she would support him, brace him, and make up for the weakness in his left leg. Winter helped James overcome his fear of falling in public venues and having to ask strangers to help him get back up.

Winter has since retired as a service dog and lives with him as a four-legged friend and confidante. His new service dog, Ares, has taken over where Winter left off. Both dogs are his hope and joy.

James is dedicated to *Dog's* Nation and its mission to give back to soldiers who have given their lives for our freedom. Like me, he sees so much potential for *Dog's Nation*. He states, "I know in my heart if it weren't for Shawn, *Dog's Nation*, and the Battle Buddy Program, I would have given up when I was stuck in that wheelchair. These dogs and the lives they save, including mine, is why I have dedicated myself to the training program and *Dog's Nation*. Shawn started something that gives hope to those who believe they have none. I have seen the impact the service dogs make on their handlers, the light that comes back into their darkness, and the miracles too numerous to count!

No matter what happens, I want to make sure the program continues. The lives saved, man and canine alike, are the mission, and it's important not to allow it to die."

EPILOGUE
About Dog's Nation

Dog's Nation is a Missouri-based non-profit, 501 (c) organization, founded by Shawn Abell in 2009. Its mission is to train rescued dogs to become service dogs for veterans, disabled children, and persons affected by autism. While Shawn works with a variety of breeds, her passion is pit bulls and pit bull mixes. "Pit bulls make great service dogs because they are low maintenance, not too large to manage, and their temperament is the best," Shawn says.

Shawn has combined her love for rescue dogs and individuals with special needs through her foundation. She has saved hundreds of dogs from coast to coast and around the world from brutal conditions and euthanasia. She then trains them to perform specific life-saving and life-enhancing tasks. Dogs once considered worthless become highly-trained service dogs which could range in cost from $25K-40K. Shawn, though, considers their lives priceless and matches them, free of cost, to deserving men, women, and children diagnosed with autism spectrum disorder, PTSD, as well as others with physical, mental, and emotional needs.

Dog's Nation is located in El Dorado Springs, a small rural community in west-central Missouri. The county has no official animal services so Shawn set up a rescue, *Dog's Nation*. Other than a few volunteers, Shawn is responsible for the care of feeding, watering, cleaning pens, and training every animal who comes into her care. She also finances the operation, the costs of which are significant.

If you would like to learn more about *Dog's Nation* or help as a volunteer or donor, please visit their website at:

https://www.facebook.com/DogsNation

Shawn Abell

Shawn's family is part of a long line of brave men who served their county in various wars, from the Missouri Volunteer regiment which served in the Civil War to her own two sons who served in the United States Armed Forces. Her son William was deployed to Iraq in 2004, 2007, 2009, and Afghanistan in 2011.

Her father served in the U.S. Army Air Corps during WWII.

Her grandfather, Walter Wesley Goddard, served in the United States Navy aboard a Patrol Torpedo boat - a torpedo-armed fast attack vessel -

during World War II and gave his life in the line of duty. He died July 4th, 1942 at the U.S. Naval Hospital in Pensacola, Florida. The family was honored with a letter of gratitude for his service signed by Franklin Roosevelt who was president of the United States of America at that time.

Her family's service has fostered strong feelings of appreciation for all the men and women who fight for our country and for our freedom. Those sentiments led her to found *Dog's Nation* in order to help veterans in need. Each dog she trains and gifts to a veteran provides support, greater self-sufficiency, offers more coping skills, decreases anxiety and stress thus reducing the risk of suicide, and improves their quality of life.

She currently resides in Missouri.

Author Renée Vajko Srch

Born to an American father and a British mother, Renée Vajko Srch grew up in France where she obtained her French Baccalaureate. She attended IBME in Switzerland, graduating with a degree in Theology. She is a speaker with Stars for Autism, educating and training individuals and businesses about autism.

She currently lives in the Missouri Ozarks with her husband and three sons, one of whom has been diagnosed with Asperger's. She is a connoisseur of fine chocolates, loves to read, and has a weakness for rescue cats.

She is a staff-writer for Herald and Banner Press. Several of her articles have been published in the Missouri Autism Report magazine. Two of her stories have been published in *Chicken Soup for the Soul* books. She also authors a blog on autism, motherhood and God. Her first novel, *Hope for Joshua,* has been accepted for publication and will be available in print and e-format later this year. She translated two autism books for children authored by Dr. Linda Barboa and Jan Luck, into French. She is currently writing a devotional for autism and special-needs families, as well as several books for children about special-needs.

You can follow her on Facebook (Author Renée Vajko Srch), Twitter (Renée Srch@SrchRenee), Pinterest (MotherhoodAutismAndGod), and Instagram (Renée Vajko Srch). She blogs at: www.MotherhoodAutismAndGod.blogspot.com

CPSIA information can be obtained
at www.ICGtesting.com
Printed in the USA
LVHW080616080620
657648LV00020B/1820